C000184411

We must welcome these friendly visitors from abroad not only for economic reasons but even more so because this leads to greater understanding and mutual appreciation. There is nothing that the world needs today more than this mutual understanding.

— *Jawaharlal Nehru.*

EASY
hindi
FOR THE TOURIST

JAICO PUBLISHING HOUSE

Ahmedabad Bangalore Bhopal Chennai
Delhi Hyderabad Kolkata Mumbai

Published by Jaico Publishing House
A-2 Jash Chambers, 7-A Sir Phirozshah Mehta Road
Fort, Mumbai - 400 001
jaicopub@jaicobooks.com
www.jaicobooks.com

© Jaico Publishing House

EASY HINDI FOR THE TOURIST
ISBN 81-7224-319-7

First Jaico Impression: 1996
Fifteenth Jaico Impression: 2009

Printed by
Sanman & Co.
113, Shivshakti Ind. Estate, Marol Naka
Andheri (E), Mumbai - 400 059.

INTRODUCTION TO "HINDUSTANI FOR THE TOURIST"

You are about to visit India, that fabled land of centuries old temples, elephants, bazaars, jungles and jewelled palaces. Sunsets that have to be seen to be believed. Rivers and snow-topped mountains that leave you breathless with awe. Houseboats on placid world-famed waters where you can live a life of leisure in palatial surroundings attended by a retinue of servants ever on your doorstep to carry out and fulfil your slightest wish. Vast distances over which you can be carried in a matter of hours by modern jet-propelled aeroplanes. If you prefer a more leisured mode of travel, there are the railways where you can have at your disposal airconditioned compartments each with its own toilet, shower and considered amongst the best in the world.

India has to be seen to be believed A lot of people think sight-seeing is boring, but not in India. The incredible wealth of monuments, temples, palaces, each one is different and must be seen to be believed. In India you will find the most modern of air-conditioned hotels, some with refrigerators in every room and all with the most wonderful views, while the standard of service and cuisine cannot be excelled anywhere. There are attractive restaurants, swimming pools and hot sunshine; in fact everything you want to make the perfect holiday.

AVOID EMBARRASSMENT

When touring India you will see something of its teeming billions and, unless you can make yourself understood, you may find yourself on innumerable occasions, slightly embarrassed! It is to reduce such occasions to a minimum that "Easy Hindi for The Tourist" will help. Your enjoyment of your travels will be greatly enhanced when you find you can make yourself understood, while the local resident and Indian will be greatly flattered that you, a visitor and tourist, can address him in his own language. Don't let yourself be misled by the advice of your friends at home or by those who have previously visited India when they say "You'll get along easily with English, why worry about Hindustani". This may have been partly true decades ago, but not today. India, like all other countries, is constantly on the change, and once the tourist gets off the "beaten track" as he will do assuredly if he is to discover the real charms of the country, then he will find a working knowledge of colloquial Hindustani to be absolutely invaluable.

BEFORE YOU LAND

Before you leave for India, preferably a week or so before your departure, you should obtain your copy of "Hindustani for the Tourist" which is available from all Tourist Offices, Airlines, and leading Booksellers throughout the world. Commence familiarising yourself with its contents. As you travel to and fro, consult it as frequently as possible, and the immediate results will be astounding. You will find yourself soon fluent enough to make yourself readily understood. You will be amazed how quickly you can acquire a working knowledge of colloquial Hindustani and when you arrive eventually in India you will find yourself competent to ask questions without hesitancy.

To simplify ready reference, all chapters in the book have been broken down to deal with almost all situations that are likely to arise or be encountered. These are indexed under "Contents". Reference there to the Page number will provide you with the required word or phrase that you may want to use in a matter of moments.

TO MAKE YOURSELF UNDERSTOOD

To help you overcome pronunciation difficulties, we have printed on the following pages throughout the book, a simple phonetic rendition of each Hindustani word, phrase or sentence in Italics. First you have the word, phrase or sentence in English. Directly underneath this is the Hindi translation in Roman letters and underneath these in the third line, you have the phonetic sound of this Hindi translation printed for you in clear Italics. Do not be afraid to pronounce all these words, phrases and sentences EXACTLY as printed in Italics and the average Indian will understand you. Take as an example the expression in English "Come here". The Hindi translation for this is "Idhar Ao". Pronounced phonetically in English this sounds as "Iddar-aow" with the "aow" pronounced as in "cow". The phonetic pronunciation is of paramount importance, so to help readers get off on the "right foot" we commence the book by giving you the "phonetic sound" values of the vowels, followed by the consonants. Then follows a Basic Vocabulary. This should be learned by heart as you will find it most useful in everyday conversation.

REMEMBER THIS

No attempt is made in this book to teach the grammar or Hindustani. The phrases which have been chosen for their versatility and applicability in meeting the needs which experience has shown to be most important, are complete in themselves and can be used WITHOUT a knowledge of grammar. By their frequent use and repetition the reader will absorb much of the grammatical structure of Hindustani. The gender of the nouns will be mastered, the ear familiarized with the sounds and the tongue with their formation.

When using the transcription, read the phrases slowly, pausing very slightly where the phonetic word has been hyphenated.

PASSPORTS AND VISAS

Citizens of the British Commonwealth do not require a visa, but they should have their passports endorsed when about to visit India. Nationals of other countries DO require valid passports AND visas.

Visas may be obtained from Indian representatives abroad and most Consular Offices. Such visa is normally valid for three months from the date of issue and for a single journey only. For those visiting the country as Tourists, they should apply for a Tourist Visa, which entitles them to special privileges in regard to registration formalities. They should also obtain a special Tourist Introduction Card. This ensures the procuration of a Liquor Permit and preferment when seeking accommodation in Government-owned Resthouses, etc. Although Tourist Visas are issued for a stay of three months in the first instance, this period can be extended to six months upon application to the Regional Registration Offices situated in all the larger cities. Tourists holding Tourist Visas must register with the police AFTER 30 days stay in India. After Registration, changes of address must be reported to the Police Registration Authorities.

WHAT YOU CAN BRING

Tourists are permitted the import of Personal
Baggage free of Customs Duty provided these
are re-exported when the tourist leaves the
country. Among the special facilities allowed
to tourists mention may be made of the following items which they may bring with them,
free of duty: Two cameras; one pair binocu-
lars; one portable wireless receiving set; one
portable record player with ten records; one
portable sound-recording apparatus; one portable musical instrument; one portable typewriter; one tent and camping gear and equipment; two watches and supporting equipment
which may include fishing gear; sporting firearms; one canoe provided it is not longer than
5 1/2 metres; one pair skis and two tennis
racquets. 200 cigarettes; 50 cigars; 250 grammes
tobacco; one bottle wine; 1/8 bottle of spirits;
1/4 litre of toilet water and a reasonable quantity of perfumes, cosmetics and medicines if
they are for personal use. In addition, tourists
may bring in ADDITIONAL quantities in excess of this quantity on an assurance that such
additional quantities will be re-exported when
they leave the country. For such additional
articles one-eighth of the usual customs duty
will be charged on such additional items. These
items which must be entered on the Re-export

Declaration Form cover two cameras in addition to the two permitted free; one extra portable wireless receiving set; one extra watch; 25 rolls of film for a still camera and 12 reels of Movie Film (8 mm. and 16 mm. only) and 300 cartridges. Husband and wife travelling together are entitled to the above concessions separately, but not so any children who may be accompanying them. Tourists importing firearms for their private use MUST obtain a Possession Licence from the Commissioner of Police at all the larger cities or better still, from the authorities at the port of disembarkation. THIS IS MOST IMPORTANT. Certain weapons are prohibited, and under this classification come (1) .303 rifles, rifles of any other bore containing parts which are interchangeable with rifles of .303 bore; (2) .410 muskets; (3) Pistols or revolvers above .32 bore.

Contents

KEY TO PRONUNCIATION

For the tourist's convenience and easy readability the vowel and consonant values as set out in the key underneath have been incorporated into the phonetic pronunciation of the translation. For those who wish to perfect their Hindi, a close study of the vowel values will be doubly rewarding.

Each vowel and a consonant used in the phonetic writing has a definite value. It represents one and one sound only. For learning the pronunciation of Hindustani, you should bear in mind each letter used in the phonetic writing and the sound which is represented by it. Those Hindustani vowels and consonants which can be illustrated by similar sounds in the English language, are given in the following list. The pronunciation of remaining letters used in the phonetic writing is explained later.

(1) Vowels.

a	as in	again	o	as in	old
a	" "	father	u	" "	put
e	" "	late	u	" "	soon
i	" "	fit,sit	ai	" "	aisle
i	" "	fatigue, machine	ao	" "	cow

(2) Consonants

k	as in	skin, act	m	as in	mud
g	" "	game	y	" "	yard
ch	" "	church	r	" "	run
j	" "	jam	l	" "	lip
t	" "	tomato, stick	v	" "	vine
d	" "	deal	w	" "	we
th	" "	thick	sh	" "	she
d	" "	they	s	" "	see
p	" "	spin, put	z	" "	zebra
b	" "	ball	h	" "	he
n	" "	net	f	" "	fan

(3) The Remaining Consonants.

(*i*) 't' is pronounced by touching the tip of the tongue to the back part of the upper teeth. "t" in "take" has the same sound when it is pronounced in this manner.

(*ii*) Try to pronounce 'r' with the tip of the tongue as in the pronunciation of 't' in 'took'.

(*iii*) Kh, gh, ch, jh, th, dh, dh, ph, bh, and rh are aspirated sounds. p, for example in spin, is an unaspirated sound, but ph is an aspirated p. In the pronunciation of ph, p is immediately followed by an outbrust of air or puff of breath as occurring in blowing the candle. Such sounds are called aspirated sounds. th in thick is an aspirated sound of t. Similarly, kh is an aspirated k, gh is an aspirated g, etc.

The following points regarding the phonetic spellings should also be noted :-

(a) 'aa' or 'ah' is pronounced as 'a' in 'father'.

(b) The 'n' in 'hn' and 'ng' has the pronunciation as a nasal twang. It shows that the preceding vowel is a nasalized vowel.

(c) 'ao' and 'aow' are pronounced as 'ow' in 'cow'.

(iv) The peculiar consonants of Hindustani which have no counterparts in English, are omitted in the phonetic spellings. Instead of these, the other consonants nearest in pronunciation which te foreigners can pronounce easily, are used.

A vowel with a nasal twang is called a nasalized vowel, e.g. 'a' in 'man' is a nasalized vowel in comparison with 'a' in 'bad' which is non-nasalized.

A HYPHEN '-' IN THE PHONETIC SPELLING SHOWS THE DIVISION OF SYLLABLES IN WORDS, WHERE YOU SHOULD HAVE A SLIGHT PAUSE IN PRONUNCIATION.

It costs nothing to be polite and the tourist would do well always to use the expression "Please" when making enquiries, issuing instructions, etc.

Please
Meharbani karke
Mayher - Baanee - Karkay

In most of the sections throughout the Phrase Book, the word "Please" has been omitted, nevertheless, the tourist should always add and use this word whenever possible. For this reason, the phonetic pronunciation should be memorised throroughly so that it can be quoted without reference.

THE BASIC VOCABULARY

Who?
Kaun?
Cawn?

What ?
Kyã ?
Kay-aah ?

When ?
Kab ?
Kab ?

How ?
Kaisa ?
Kai-sah ?

Why ?
Kyon ?
Queon ?

Where ?
Kidhar ?
Kiddar ?

There
Udhar
Uddar

Here
Idhar
Iadar

No
Nahin; na
Na-heehn; na

Yes
Hãn
Hahn

Inside
Andar
Under

Outside
Bãhar
Bah-her

Less
Kam
Come

More
Zyãdã
Zey-add-ah

Quickly
Jaldí
Juldy

Soon
Jaldí
Juldy

Often
Aksar
Ak-sar

How much ?
Kitnã
Kit-nah ?

Thank you
Shukriyā
Shook-ree-yah

Please
Meharbāni karke
Mayher-baanee karkay

How are you ?
Ap kaise hain ?
Aap kai-say highn ?

All right
Achchhā
Atch-chah

That much
Utnā
Oot-nah

As much
Jitnā
Jit-nah

Whose ?
Kiskā ?
Kiss-kah ?

How long ?
Kitnā lambā ?
Kit-nah lumbah ?

Excuse me
Māf karnā
Maaf-kar-nah

Please repeat
Meharbāni karke
phir boliye
*Mayherbaanee karkay
fear bowl-ee-eh*

How do you do ?
Ap kaise hain ?
Aap kai-say highn ?

Good bye
Achchhā
Atch-chah

Whom ?
Kisko ?
Kiss-ko?

How many ?
Kitne ?
Kit-nay ?

How big ?
Kitnā barā ?
Kit-nah burrah?

Good day, good morning, good afternoon,
good night
Namaste (said politely and mostly with joined
hands)
Naam-astay

PRONOUNS

I	We
Main	Ham
Maiyn	*Hum*
Thou	**You**
Tú	Tum; Ãp (showing
Too	respect)
	Toom; Aap
He, She, It	**They**
Voh	Ve
Voh	*Way*

Tú 'Thou' is generally not used in calling some one, because in such context it implies the sense of disrespect. Ham and Tum are often used for 'I' and 'Thou' respectively.

PRONOUNS WITH USEFUL VERBS

I am	We are
Main hún	Ham hain
Mayn hoohn	*Hum highn*
Thou art	**You are**
Tú hai	Tum ho
Too high (Toom)	*Toom ho*
He, She, It is	**They are**
Voh hai	Ve hain
Voh hai	*Way highn*

Was	Were
Thã (M) ; Thí (F)	The (M); Thin (F)
Thah ; Tee	*Thay; Teehn*
I was	**We were**
Main thã (M) ;	Ham the (M);
Main thí (F)	Ham thi (F)
Mayn thah; Mayn tee	*Hum thay; Hum tee*
You were	**They were**
Tum the (M); Tum	Ve the (M); Ve
thin (F)	thin (F)
Toom thay; Toom teehn	*Way thay; Way*
He was	*teehn*
Voh thã	**She was**
Voh thah	Voh thí
	Voh tee

POSSESSIVE PRONOUNS

My	His, hers , its
Merã (M); Merí (F)	Uskã (M) ; Uskí (F)
May-rah ; May-ree	*Ooskah ; Ooskee*
Thy	**Our**
Terã (M); Terí (F)	Hamãrã (M);
Tay-rah; Tay-ree	Hamãrí (F)
	Ha-ma-rah; Ha-ma-ree

ALL ABOUT YOURSELF

My name is............
Merã nãm .... hai.
May-rah naam ....high.

It is spelt like this
Yah is tarah likhã jatã hai.
Ya iss tarah likha ja-tah high.

I am a citizen of ....
Main .... kã rahane vãlã hún.
Maiyn ... kah ra-ha-nay waalah hoohn.

I am thirty years old.
Main tís sãl kã hún.
Maiyn teese saal kah hoohn.

My permanent address is ...
Merã dãyami patã yah hai.
May-rah dad-imee patah ya high.

I have come from....
Main ... se ãyã hún.
Maiyn ..... say ayah hoohn.

I bank with Lloyds Bank.
Merã hisãb-kitãb 'Lloyds Bank' men hai.
May-rah hisaab-kitaab 'Lloyds Bank' mayn high.

My passport number is ....
Merã 'passport number' ... hai.
May-rah 'passport number' ....high.

It was issued at .... on ....
Yah ... men ... tãríkh ko nikãlã gayã hai.
Ya ...mayn ...tah-reek ko nikah-lah gayah high.

12

It is valid upto
  Yah .... tak chalegã .
  Ya .... tuck challay-gah.

I am married .
  Main shãdi shudã hún.
  Maiyn shaadee-shoodah hoohn.

I am a bachelor.
  Main kunãrã hún.
  Maiyn Coohn-arah hoohn.

I have come to see relatives.
  Main rishtedãron ko dekhne 'ãyã hún.
  Main rishtay-daarohn ko deck-nay ayah hoohn.

Do I register with the authorities ?
  Main police ke pãs nãm dãkhil karãún.
  Maiyn police kay pass naam dah-kill karah-oohn?

I weigh 82 kilos.
  Merã vazan bayãsí kilo hai.
  May-rah wazan bay-ah-see kilo high.

CUSTOMS ON YOUR ARRIVAL .

Do I fill in any forms ?
 Mujhe kuchh 'form' bharne hain kyã ?
 Moojay kootch 'form' burr-nay highn kay-aah ?
Where do I get them from ?
 Ve mujhe kidhar se milenge ?
 Way moojay kiddar say mill-engay ?
What need I declare ?
 Mujhe kyã batãnã chãhiye ?
 Moojay kay-aah bat-annah chah-he-eh ?
Where is the customs checkpoint ?
 Customs-vãle kidhar jãnch karte hain ?
 Customs-wallay kiddar jaanch kartay highn ?
Can I import alcohol ?
 Main sharãb lã sakta hún kyã ?
 Maiyn shar-aab lah suck-tah hoohn kay-aah ?
This is my health certificate.
 Yah merí tandurustí kã pramãn-patra hai.
 Ya may-ree tand-roostee kah pramaan-patra high

This is my passport.
> Yah merā 'passport' hai.
> *Ya may-rah 'passport' high.*

I am a tourist.
> Main sailānī hún.
> *Maiyn sailaanee hoohn.*

I am a businessman.
> Main vyāpāri hún.
> *Maiyn vee-ah-paaree hoohn.*

These are my bags.
> Yah merā sāmān hai.
> *Ya may-rah saamaan high.*

These are all my personal effects.
> Ye sab mere shakhsí kām ke liye hain.
> *Ye sub may-ray shak-see kaam kay-lee-eh highn.*

I have nothing to declare.
> Mere pās aisí koí chíz nahín, jo batāni chāhiye .
> *May-ray pass ai-see ko-ee cheese na-heehn, jo bat-annee chah-he-eh.*

Are these things dutiable ?
> Kyā is chízen par kar denā paregā ?
> *Kay-aah iss cheese-ehn per cur they-nah per-eh-ga?*

How much duty must I pay ?
> Kitnā kar denā paregā ?
> *Kit-nah cur they-nah per-eh-ga ?*

Bring my bags here.
> Merā sāmān idhar lāo.
> *May-rah saamaan iddar laow.*

Shall I open these ?

  Main yah kholún kyã ?

  Maiyn ya kol-oohn kay-aah ?

This contains personal...

  Is men sab merí shaksí chízen hain.

  Iss mayn sub may-ree shak-see cheese-ehn highn.

Take my bag there.

  Merã sãmãn udhar le jão .

  May-rah saamaan uddar lay-jaow.

May I close them now ? (Close it ?)

  Main ab yah band karún kyã? (Band karún?)

  Maiyn ab ya bund karoohn kay-aah ? (Bund karoohn ?)

Where I can get change ?

  Mujhe rezgí kidhar-se milegí ?

  Moojay rays-gee kiddar say mill-eh-gee ?

Is there a toilet anywhere near ?

  Hãth-munh dhone kã kamrã nazdík hai kyã ?

  Haat-moohn doe-nay kah come-rah naz-deek high kay-aah ?

Where is it then ?

  Phir kidhar hai ?

  Fear kiddar high ?

Is there a tourist office here ?

  Sailãniyon kã daftar idhar hai kyã ?

  Sailannee-ohn kah daftar iddar high kay-aah ?

Can I get there by bus ?

Main udhar 'bus' se jã saktã hún kyã ?

Maiyn uddar 'bus' say ja suck-tah hoohn kay-aah?

How far is it to town ?

Voh shahar se kitnã dúr hai ?

Voh sha-her say kit-nah doo-r high ?

Can I get a carriage here ?

Idhar mujhe garí mil sajtí hai kyã ?

Iddar moojay gar-ree mill suck-tee high kay-aah ?

Call me a taxi (please).

Mere liye 'taxi' bulão.

May-ray lee-eh 'taxi' bull-aow (as in "cow").

Take me to a good hotel.

Mujhe kisí achchhe 'hotel' men le chalo.

Moojay kissee atch-chay 'hotel' mayn lay challo.

One in the middle of the town preferred.

Shahar ke bích men ho, to achchhã.

Sha-her kay beach mayn ho, toe atch-chah.

Take me there (please).

Mujhe udhar le chalo.

Moojay uddar lay challo.

I wish to go to ....

Main ... jãnã chahitã hún.

Maiyn ... ja-nah chah-ha-tah hoohn.

AT YOUR HOTEL, RESTHOUSE, OR DAK BUNGALOW

Most hotels in the larger tourist centres are completely modern and offer all amenities. Off the beaten track (and this is where the tourist must go if he is to see the best that the country offers) the Resthouse or Dak Bungalow will be the place where he will stay. These are usually former private residences each with its own compound (garden, walks, etc.). Normally one makes reservations in advance to ensure accommodation. There is to be found always at least one servant in residence, sometimes more. These, at the very shortest of notices will conjure up an appetizing meal, in a manner that reminds one of Alladin's Lamp! The charges for the use of these Resthouses and Bungalows is very moderate. In them, one can sit back and relax in complete safety even in the wildest surroundings. Where mosquitoes are prevalent, nets for the beds are usually provided, but for their personal comfort, most tourists provide themselves with an anti-mosquito cream or lotion, obtainable at almost all chemist shops.

Have you a reservation for me ?
Ãp-ne mere liye jagah rakhí hai ?
Aap-nay may-ray lee-eh jug-ah ruck-key high ?

I wired you two weeks ago.
Main-ne do hafte pahale ãp ko tãr bhejã thã
Maiyn-nay doe huff-tay pie-lay aap-ko taar bedge-ah tah.

Have you a single room ?
Ãp ke pãs ek ãdmí ke rahane kã kamarã hai?
Aap-kay pass ek aad-me kay rahanay kah come-rah high ?

Have you a double room with single beds?
Ãpke pãs do ãdmiyon kã kamrã alag alag bistar se hai ?
Aap-kay pass doe ad-me-ohn kah come-rah alag alag bister say high ?

I want one with a bathroom.
Mujhe ghusal khāne ke sath kamarā chāhiye.
Moojay goosal kah-nay kay saat come-rah chah-he-eh.

I do not require a private bathroom.
Mujhe khāngi ghusal-khānā nahín chāhiye.
Moojay kaan-gee goosal kah-nah naheehn chah-he-eh.

How much is it ?
Is ke kitne paise hain ?
Iss-kay kit-nay pice-eh highn ?

Does that include meals ?
Is men khānā bhí miltā hai ?
Iss mayn kah-nah bee mill-tah high ?

How much is it without meals ?
Khāne ke sivā kitne paise hain ?
Kah-nay kay sivah kit-nay pice-eh highn ?

For myself and my wife.
Mere aur meri aurat ke liye.
May-ray owr may-ree ow-rut kay lee-eh.

For a party of three.
Tín logon ke liye.
Teen low-gohn kay ice-eh.

For myself only.
Sirf mere liye.
Sirf may-ray lee-eh.

For one night only.
Sirf ek rāt ke liye.
Sirf ek raat kay lee-eh.

For a few days perhaps.
Shāyad kuchchh dinon ke liye.
Shah-yad kootch dinohn kay lee-eh.

I am not sure for how long.
Mālúm nahín kab tak.
Ma-loom na-heehn cub-tuck.

It is rather expensive.
Yah mahengā hai.
Ya ma-heng-ah high.

Have you anything cheaper ?
Is-se sastā hai ?
Iss-say sus-tah high ?

Show me the room.
Mujhe kamarā dikhāo.
Moojay come-rah dick-aow.

It is too small.
Yah babut chhotā hai.
Ya ba-hoot chotah high.

It is too big.
Yah bahut barā hai.
Ya ba-hoot burrah high.

It has no view.
Is-se nazārā nahín díkhtā.
Iss-say nazah-rah na-heehn deeck-tah.

It is too noisy.
Is men bahut shor hai.
Iss mayn ba-hoot shore high.

It is too hot.
Yah bahut garam hai.
Ya ba-hoot gar-rum high.

It is very draughty.
Is men bahut havā ātí hai.
Iss mayn ba-hoot hawah ah-tea high.

I want a quiet room.
Mujhe ekānt-wālā kamarā chāhiye.
Moojay ek-aunt waalah come-rah chah-he-eh.

There is no fresh air here.
Idhar tāzí havā nahín hai.
Iddar taazee hawah na-heehn high.

It is very dirty.
Yah bahut gandā hai.
Ya ba-hoot gun-dah high.

Do the fans work ?
Pankhe chalte hain ?
Pung-kay chall-tay highn ?

How much extra for an airconditioned room ?
'Air-conditioned' kamre ke liye kitne paise zyādā lete hai ?
'Air-conditioned' come-ray kay lee-eh kit-nay pice-eh zey-add-ah lay-tay highn ?

I shall take it.
Mujhe yah chāhiye.
Moojay ya chah-he-eh.

(Please) give me the key ?
Mujhe chābí díjiye.
Moojay chah-bee thee-jee-eh.

Open the windows.
Khirkiyān kholo.
Kir-key-yaan ko-low.

Can I deposit valuables here ?
Main kímatí chízen idhar amānat rakhún ?
Maiyn key-mat-tea cheese-ehn iddar amah-nut ruck-hoohn ?

Here is my key.
Merí chābí lo.
May-ree chah-bee low.

Is there a barber here ?
Idhar hajjam hai ?
Iddar hajaam high.

Can I engage a reliable servant here ?
Mujhe idhar ímāndār naukar mil saktā hai ?
Moojay iddar eemaan-dar now-ker mill suck-tah high ?

Can I have my linen cleaned here ?
Main apne kapre idhar dhulā saktā hùn ?
Maiyn up-nay cup-ray iddar doolah suck-tah hoohn?

How far away is the shopping centre ?
Bāzār kitnā dúr hai ?
Bazaar kit-nah doo-r high ?

Where is the dressing room?
Kapre badalne kā kamarā kidhar hai ?
Cup-ray bud-dull-nay kah come-rah kiddar high ?

Do you supply early morning tea ?
Āp subah ko chay dete hain ?
Aap soobah ko chah they-tay highn ?

At what time are meals served ?
Khānā kitne baje miltā hai ?
Kah-nah kit-nay budge-eh mill-tah high ?

Can I have meals in my room ?
Khānā mere kamre men mil saktā hai ?
Kah-nah may-ray come-ray mayn mill suck-tah high ?

I am a vegetarian.
Main shākāhārí hún.
Maiyn shaak-ah-haare hoohn.

Do you charge extra for that ?
Kyā, āp iske liye zyādā paise lete hai ?
Kay-aah aap iss-kay lee-eh zey-add-ah pice-eh lay-tay highn ?

How much extra ?
Kitne paise zyādā ?
Kit-nay pice-eh zey-add-ah ?

Are there dress regulations ?

Poshāk ke liye idhar kāide hain kyā ?

Poe-shaak kay lee-eh iddar kah-ee-they highn kay-aah ?

Can I dine in shorts at lunch ?

Main nekar pahan kar dopahar kā khānā khā saktā hún ?

Maiyn nicker pahan-ker doe-pahar kah kah-nah kah suck-tah hoohn ?

Can I bring ladies to my room ?

Auraton ko apne kamre men lā saktā hún ?

Ow-rut-ohn ko up-nay come-ray mayn lah suck-tah hoohn ?

Is there a cabaret ?

Idhar "cabaret" hai ?

Iddar "cabaret" high ?

What is the admission fee ?

Dākhilā-fee kitní hai ?

Dah-kill-ah fee kit-nee high ?

Can I get drinks in my room ?

Píne kí chízen mujhe apne kamre men mil saktí hain ?

Pee-nay key cheese-ehn moojay up-nay come-ray mayn mill suck-tea high ?

Where is the bar ?

"Bar" kidhar hai ?

'Bar' kiddar high ?

I wish to be called at five.

Mujhe panch baje bulaya jae.

Moojay pahnch budge-eh bull-ayah ja-eh.

(Please) have a taxi waiting for me..

Mere liye 'taxi' thaharāo.

May-ray lee-eh 'taxi' tie-raow. ("Ow" as in "cow")

Any message for me ?

Mere liye koí paighām hai ?

May-ray lee-eh ko-ee pie-gaam high ?

Any callers for me ?

Mere liye koí mulākātí āyā hai kyā ?

May-ray lee-eh ko-ee mool-ah-ka-tea ayah high kay-aah ?

If anyone calls say I shall be back for lunch.

Agar koí bulāe, to kahanā ki main dopahar ko khāne ke vakt lautúngā.

Agar ko-ee bull-ah-eh, toe ka-ha-nah key maiyn doe-pahar ko kah-nay kay wakt laow-toohn-gah.

(Please) send the bearer to my room.

Baire ko mere kamre men bhejiye.

Bai-ray ko may-ray come-ray mayn bedge-ee-eh.

I am expecting a visitor.

Merā mulākātí āne wālā hai.

May-rah mool-ah-kah-tea ah-nay wall-ah high.

When he comes show him to my room.

Jab voh āe to use me.e kamre men bhejnā.

Jub voh ah-eh toe oosay r̄ay-ray come-ray mayn bedge-nah.

I wish to speak to the manager.

Main 'Manager' se bolnā chāhatā hún.

Maiyn 'Manager' say bowl-nah chah-ha-tah hoohn.

I shall be leaving on Wednesday.

Main budh-wār ko jāúgā.

Maiyn bood-war ko ja-oongah.

Kindly forward my mail to the address.

Merí dāk mere pate par bhejnā.

May-ree dak may-ray patay per bedge-nah.

Is there a travel agency near ?

'Travel Agency' nazdík hai ?

'Travel Agency' naz-deek high ?

Is room service included ?

Kamre men pahunchāne ke paise bhí is men hain kyā ?

Come-ray mayn pa-hoohn-chah-nay kay pice-eh bee iss-mayn highn kay-aah ?

The lock does not work.

Tālā thík nahín hai.

Tah-lah teak na-heehn high.

Bring another blanket.
  Dusrā kambal lāo.
  Doosrah come-bal laow.

I want these shoes polished.
  Mera juta 'polish' karo.
  May-rah jute-ah 'polish' karo.

Is there a plug for razors ?
  Dārhí ke "razor" ke liye idhar 'plug' hai ?
  Dah-ree kay 'razor'kay lee-eh iddar 'plug' high ?

What is the room number ?
  Kamre ka 'number' kyā hai ?
  Come-ray kah 'number' kay-aah high ?

(Please) Send a messenger up.
  Kāsid ko úpar bhejiye.
  Kah-sid ko ooper bedge-ee-eh.

I think you have made an error.
  Main samajhtā hún tum-ne ghalatí kí hai.
  Maiyn sumaj-tah hoohn toom-nay gull-tea key high.

Are there resthouses there ?
  Udhar ārām-ghar hain ?
  Uddar aaraam-ghar highn ?

What do they charge ?
  Ve kitne paise lete hain ?
  Way kit-nay pice-eh lay-tay highn ?

Can you get food there ?
Tumko udhar khānā mil saktā hai ?
Tcom-ko uddar kah-nah mill suck-tah high ?

Are they safe to sleep in ?
Udhar sone men salāmatí hai ?
Uddar so-nay mayn salah-mattee high ?

Is there a bungalow near ?
Udhar banglā nazdík hai ?
Uddar bung-law naz-deek high ?

Can we stay a long time ?
Udhar ham bahut wakt thahar sakte hain ?
Uddar hum ba-hoot wakt tie-her suck-tay highn ?

Must we book in advance ?
Jagah rakhne ke liye, pahale hí likhnā
zarúrí hai kyā ?
*Jugah ruck-nay kay lee-eh, pie-lay he lick-nah
zarooree high kay-aah ?*

Is it far off ?
Voh bahut dúr hai kyā ?
Voh ba-hoot doo-r high kay-aah ?

How do we get there ?
Ham udhar kis tarah jā sakte hain ?
Hum uddar kiss tarah ja suck-tay highn ?

Can you show us the way ?
Āp rāstā dikhā sukte hain ?
Aap raastah dick-ah suck-tay highn ?

Where does this lead to ?
Yah rāstā k.dhar jātā hai ?
Ya raastah kiddar ja-tah high ?

Can we walk ?
Hum paidal jā sakte hain ?
Hum pie-dull ja suck-tay highn ?

Is it safe to bathe here ?
Idhar ghusal karne men salāmatí hai?
Iddar goosal kar-nay maiyn salah-mattee high ?

Is there electric light ?
Udhar bijlí hai ?
Uddar bij-lee high ?

Do they supply bedding ?
Ve bistar dete hain ?
Way bister they-tay highn ?

Do they supply linen ?
Ve kapre dete hain ?
Way cup-ray they-tay highn ?

Is there a cook ?
Udhar khānā banāne wālā hai ?
Uddar kah-nah bunah-nay wallah high ?

Does he buy the food ?
Voh khānā kharíd lātā hai ?
Voh kah-nah kar-eed lah-tah high ?

Can we drink the water ?
Ham pānī pí sakte hain ?
Hum paanee pea suck-tay highn ?

Do we sign the book ?
Ham kitāb par sahí karen kyã ?
Hum kitab per sahee kar-ehn kay-aah ?

How much do we pay ?
Hamko kitnã denã hogã ?
Hum ko kit-nah they-nah hogah ?

Do they expect gratuities ?
Ve inām chāhate hain kyã ?
Way inaam chah-ha-tay highn kay-aah ?

About how much ?
Lag bhag kitnã ?
Lug bhag kit-nah ?

Can our servant sleep here ?
Hamārā naukar idhar so saktā hai ?
Hum-ah-rah now-kar iddar so suck-tah high ?

Can he get food ?
Use khānā mil saktā hai ?
Oosay kah-nah mill suck-tah high ?

And the driver too ?
Aur 'driver' ko bhí ?
Owr 'driver' ko bee ?

USE THIS INTERNATIONAL TELEGRAPH CODE WHEN RESERVING ACCOMMODATION IN HOTELS.

Requirements	*Code*
1 room with 1 bed	Alba
1 room with 1 large bed	Aldua
1 room with 2 beds	Arab
1 room with 3 beds	Abec
2 rooms with 1 bed each	Belab
2 rooms with 3 beds	Birac
2 rooms with 2 beds each	Bonad
3 rooms with 1 bed each	Ciroc
3 rooms with 4 beds	Carid
3 rooms with 2 beds each	Caduf
4 rooms with 1 bed each	Danid
4 rooms with 2 beds each	Diroh
Child's bed	Kind
Sitting-room	Sal
Air-conditioned accommodation	Acond
Private bathroom	Bat
Servant's room	Serv
Room with good view	Belvu
Length of stay : 1 night	Pass
Cancelling Room	Anul
Length of stay : several days	Stop
Ordinary garage for 1 Motor	Garag
Meet at Station	Train
Meet at landing	Quai

| Meet at Airport | | | | Aero |
| Meet at motorbus terminus from Airport | | | | Aeroz |

Arrival	Morning	Afternoon	Evening	Night
Sunday	Pobab	Polyp	Rabal	Ranuv
Monday	Pocun	Pomel	Racex	Rapin
Tuesday	Podyl	Ponow	Radok	Raqaf
Wednesday	Pogok	Popuf	Rafyg	Ratyz
Thursday	Pohix	Porik	Ragub	Ravup
Friday	Pojaw	Posev	Rahiv	Rawow
Saturday	Pokuz	Povah	Rajod	Raxab

This Morning	This Afternoon	This Evening	This Night
Powys	Pozum	Ramyk	Razem

SERVANTS YOU MAY NEED AND THEIR ENGAGEMENT

This is always a ticklish problem for the new-comer. References (chits) cannot always be relied upon as often an applicant will present as his personal references, chits that have been "lent" to him by an already employed servant elsewhere. This form of deception is quite common, particularly in up-country stations, and must be guarded against. Since the tenor of your future life will be regulated largely by the type of servant you engage, too much importance cannot be attached to the engagement of the right servant. The best and correct method is to engage one only that is personally recommended and known to an established travel agency or hotel. Normally servants engaged from such sources are completely reliable and the soul of honesty. Like everywhere else, of course, there are exceptions. Once engaged, it is imperative that the employer retains in his personal custody, the servant's chits or references. By so doing, a safety measure is taken that often pays dividends, as a servant will not leave your service without his chits since he cannot obtain employment elsewhere, without them.

Whether one travels or not, the tourist is well

advised to engage at least one personal servant usually known as a butler/bearer or cook/ bearer. A competent servant can save the tourist many headaches. He will provide meals, wash and valet clothes, clean shoes and look after the well-being of his employer in every sense of the term. He can plan excursions, make reservations, buy tickets, offer suggestions, and generally speaking, is worth his weight in gold. In the cities, a bearer engaged there expects a remuneration of approximately Rs. 80-120, plus batta (allowances when travelling out of station) per month. In smaller centres, the pay may be considerably lower.

Bearer.
Bairā.
Bai-rah.

Butler.
Khānsāmā.
Kaan-sah-mah.

Boy.
Chhokrā.
Choke-rah.

Cleaner.
Safāi karne-wālā .
Suf-ah-ee kar-nay-wall-ah.

Driver.
Driver.
Driver.

Nannie.
Āya.
Ayah.

Sweeper (male).
Mehtar; Hamal.
May-ier; Hum-all.

Sweeper (female)
Mehtarāní.
May-teranee.

What is your name?
Tumhārā nãm kyã hai ?
Toom-ha-rah naam kay-aah high ?

How old are you ?
Tum kitne sãl ke ho ?
Toom kit-nay saal kay ho ?

Can you read ?
Tum parh sakte ho ?
Toom purr suck-tay ho ?

Can you write ?
Tum likh sakte ho ?
Toom lick suck-tay ho ?

Are you honest ?
Tum ímandãr ho ?
Toom eemaan-dar ho ?

One to be trusted.
Wishwãs lãik.
Wish-wass lah-ick.

Can you speak English ?
Angrezí bol sakte ho ?
Ung-ray-zee bowl suck-tay ho ?

Do you know local languages ?
Idhar kí boliyãn jãnte ho ?
Iddar key bowl-ee-ahn jaan-tay ho ?

For whom have you worked previously ?
Tum ne pahale kiske pãs kãm kiyã hai ?
Toom-nay pie-lay kiss-kay pass kaam key-ah high?

Let me see your reference ?
   Apne sifārish-nāme dikhāo ?
   Up-nay sifa-rish-nah-may dick-aow ?

Can you cook ?
   Tum khānā banā sakte ho ?
   Toom kah-nah banah suck-tay ho ?

Are you accustomed to travel ?
   Tum musāfirī karne ke ādi ho ?
   Toom moosah-free kar-nay kay ah-dee ho ?

Do you know India well ?
   Tum Hindustān ke bāre men achchhī
   tarah jānte ho ?
   *Toom 'Hindustan' kay bah-ray mayn atch-chee
   tarah jaan-tay ho ?*

What is your religion ?
   Tumhārā dharam kyā hai ?
   Toom-ha-rah daram kay-aah high ?

Are you married or single ?
   Tum shādi-shudā ho, yā akele ho ?
   Toom shaadee-shoodah ho, ya a-kay-lay ho ?

How many in your family ?
   Tumhāre parivār men kitne log hain ?
   Toom-ha-ray pari-war mayn kit-nay log highn ?

Are you clean in person ?
   Tum apnī safāī rakhte ho ?
   Toom up-nee suf-ah-ee ruck-tay ho ?

Do you bathe daily ?
  Tum roz ghusal karte ho ?
  Toom rose goosal kar-tay ho ?

Can you press clothes ?
  Tum kapre istrí kar sakte ho ?
  Toom cup-ray iss-tree kar-suck-tay ho ?

What pay do you expect ?
  Tumhen kitní tankhwāh chāhiye ?
  Toom-hehn kit-nee ton-kah chah-he-eh ?

It is too much.
  Yah bahut zyādā hai.
  Ya ba-hoot zey-add-ah high ?

I shall give you Rs.
  Main tumhen…. rupae dúnga.
  Maiyn toom-hehn ….roopa-eh doohn-gah.

And expenses when travelling.
  Aur musāfirí kā kharchā.
  Owr moosah-free kah kar-chah.

I do not think you will suit me.
  Main samajhtā hún , tum merā kām nahín
  kar sakoge.
  *Maiyn sum-aj-tah hoohn, toom may-rah kaam
  na-heehn kar suck-o-gay.*

I shall give you a trial.
  Tumhen kām karne kā maukā detā hún.
  *Toom-hehn kaam kar-nay kah mow-kah they-
  tah hoohn.*

When can you start ?
Kab shurú karoge ?
Cub shooroo kar-oh-gay ?

Have you got clean clothing ?
Tumhen sãf kapre hain ?
Toom-hehn saaf cup-ray highn ?

You are engaged from ....
Tum ... tãríkh se kãm par ão.
Toom ....ta-reek say kaam per aow.

You can start at once.
Tum abhíse kãm shurú kar sakte ho.
Toom a-bee-say kaam shooroo kar suck-tay ho.

Come from tomorrow.
Kalse ão.
Kal-say aow.

Come from next Monday.
Dúsre Somwãr se ão.
Doos-ray Soam-war say aow.

From the first of the month.
Pahalí taríkh se.
Pie-lee ta-reek say.

DIRECTIONS TO SERVANTS

Come here.
Idhar āo.
Iddar aow.

Go there.
Udhar joā.
Uddar jaow.

Wait here.
Idhar thaharo.
Iddar tie-ro.

Speak up.
Bolo.
Bowl-oh.

Stand here ?
Idhar khare raho.
Iddar kar-eh raho.

Stand there.
Udhar khare raho.
Uddar kar-eh raho.

Stand still.
Chup khare raho.
Choop kar-eh raho.

Say it again.
Phir bolo.
Fear bowl-oh.

That will do.
Voh thik hai.
Voh teak high.

Here are my keys.
Ye hain merī chā-biyãn.
Yeh highn may-ree chah-bee-ahn.

Give them back to me.
Ve mujhe wāpas do.
Way moojay wah-pus doe.

Switch the lights on.
Battī jalāo.
But-tea jal-aow.

Light the lamps.
  Battiyãn jalão.
  But-tea-ahn jal-aow.

Open my bags (trunks)
  Merí petiyãn kholo.
  May-ree pay-tea-ahn ko-lo.

Put my things away.
  Merí chízen ander rakho.
  May-ree cheese-ehn under ruck-oh.

Get a bath ready.
  Ghusal kã sãmãn taiyãr rakho.
  Goosal kah sah-maan tie-yaar ruck-oh.

Put clean linen out.
  Sãf kapre bãhar rakho.
  Saaf cup-ray bah-har ruck-oh.

Make up my bed.
  Merã bistar taiyãr rakho.
  May-rah bister tie-yaar ruck-oh.

Spread my bedding.
  Merã bistar lagão.
  May-rah bister lug-aow.

Put it on the table.
  Yah mez par rakho.
  Ya maize per ruck-oh.

Get me some cigarettes.
  Mere liye kuchh 'cigarette' le ão.
  May-ray lee-eh kootch 'cigarette' lay aow.

Call me at seven.

Mujhe sāt baje bulāo.

Moojay saat budge-eh bull-aow.

Bring me morning tea.

Subah ko mere liye chāy lāo.

Soobah ko may-ray lee-eh chah laow.

Have my shoes cleaned.

Mere júte sāf karo.

May-ray jute-eh saaf karo.

Press these trousers.

Yah patlún istrí karo.

Ya patloon iss-tree karo.

Bring some hot water.

Thorā garam pāní lāo.

Tore-ah gar-rum paa-nee laow.

Put the lights out.

Battí band karo.

But-tea bund karo.

What is the time ?

Kitne baje hain ?

Kit-nay budge-eh highn ?

Take this note to ...

Yah chithí ... ke pās le jāo.

Ya chit-tea .... kay pas lay jaow.

Make tea.

Chāy taiyār karo.

Chah tie-yaar karo.

42

Get breakfast ready.
Nāshtā taiyār rakho.
Naash-tah tie-yaar ruck-oh.

Bring some bread.
Dabalrotí lāo.
Double-rotea laow.

Toast some bread.
Dabalrotí senko.
Double-rotea sayn-ko.

Boil two eggs medium.
Do ande madhyam ubālo.
Doe anday mud-yam oobah-lo.

I want them hard boiled.
Ye mujhe achchhí tarah ubāle hue chāhiye.
Yea moojay atch-chee tarah oobah-lay hoo-eh chah-he-eh.

This egg is not cooked properly.
Yah andā achchhí tarah nahín banāyā hai.
Ya andah atch-chee tarah na-heehn banah-yah high.

Butter the bread.
Dabalrotí ko makhan lagāo.
Double-rotea ko muckan lag-aon

Bring me a knife.
Chākú lāo.
Chah-koo laow.

Bring a fork.

Kāntā lāo.

Kahntah laow.

Bring a cup and a saucer.

Piyālā aur tashtarī lāo.

Pea-ah-lah owr tash-taree laow.

Lay the table neatly.

Mez sāf tarāh se lagāo.

Maize saaf tarah say lug-aow.

Change the table-cloth.

Mez-posh badlo.

Maize-poash budlo.

This is filthy.

Yah gandā hai.

Ya gun-dah high.

Have it washed immediately.

Yah jaldī dho dalo.

Ya juldy dough dah-lo.

Clean my room.

Merā kamra sāf karo.

May-rah come-rah saaf karo.

Bring my clothes.

Mere kapre lāo.

May-ray cup-ray laow.

Sew on this button.

Yah 'button' si lo.

Ya 'button' see lo.

Mend this sock.
Yah moza si lo.
Ya mo-zah see lo.

Remove this stain.
Yah dãgh mitão.
Ya daag mit-taow.

Polish this silver.
Yah chãndí chamkão.
Ya chahn-dee chum-kaow.

Have the room swept.
Kamrã sãf karo.
Come-rah saaf karo.

Carry out my orders.
Mere hukum kí tãmíl karo.
May-ray hookum key tah-meal karo.

Don't delay.
Der mat karo.
They-r mutt karo.

Be smart and quick.
Chust aur chãlãk bano.
Choost owr chah-laak bano.

Empty this basket.
Yah tokrí khãlí karo.
Yo tokree kah-lee karo.

Go to the bazar.
Bãzãr jão.
Bazaar jaow.

Buy me this.

Mere liye yah kharíd lão.

May-ray lee-eh ya kareed laow.

Clean it up.

Yah sãf karo.

Ya saaf karo.

You may go now.

Ab jã sakte ho.

Ab jah suck-tay ho.

Where have you been ?

Tum kidhar gaye the ?

Toom kiddar ga-eh tay ?

Stay on the premises.

Andar hí thaharo.

Under he tie-ro.

Fetch that package.

Voh band kiyã huã sãmãn idhar lão.

Voh bund key-ah hoo-ah saamaan iddar laow.

Call a porter.

Kúlí ko bulão.

Coolie ko bull-aow.

Bring the laundryman.

Dhobí ko bulão.

Doe-bee ko bull-aow.

Tell him to come.

Usko ãne ke liye bolo.

Oosko ah-nay kay lee-eh bowl-oh.

Tell him to go.

Usko bolo ki, voh chalā jāe.

Oosko bowl-oh ki, voh challah ja-eh.

Bring it immediately.

Yah jaldí lāo.

Ya juldy laow.

Don't delay. Do it now.

Der mat karo. Abhí karo.

They-r mutt karo. A-bee karo.

What is there for dinner ?

Khāne ke liye kyā hai ?

Kah-nay kay lee-eh kay-aah high ?

Order the dinner now.

Abhí khana lāne ke liye kaho.

A-bee kah-nah lah-nay kay lee-eh kah-ho.

When will it be ready ?

Voh kab taiyār hogā ?

Voh cub tie-yaar hogah ?

Bring a menu card.

Khāne kí suchí le āo.

Kah-nay key soochee lay aow.

We shall eat now.

Ham ab khāenge .

Hum ab kah-engay .

I am hungry.

Mujhe bhúkh lagí hai.

Moojay book lug-ee high.

I am thirsty.
Mujhe pyăs lagí hai.
Moojay pea-aas lug-ee high.

I am tired.
Main thakhă hua hún.
Maïn tuck-ah hoo-ah hoohn.

This knife is blunt.
Yah chaku kund hai.
Ya chah-koo koond high.

Have it sharpened.
Yah tez karão.
Ya taize karaow.

There is too much salt.
Is men bahut namak hai.
Iss-mayn ba-hoot namaak high.

Get some mustard.
Thorí răi lão.
Tore-ee rah-ee laow.

This plate is not clean.
Yah tashtarí săf nahín hai.
Ya tash-taree saaf na-heehn high.

Keep your fingers off it.
Apní anguliyăn is se dúr rakho.
Up-nee angoolee-ahn iss-say doo-r ruck-oh.

Clean the plate properly.
Tashtari achchhí tarah săf karo.
Tash-taree atch-chee tarah saaf karo.

Has this water been boiled ?
Yah pãní ubãlã gayã hai ?
Ya paanee oobah-lah gayah high ?

Are you certain about it ?
Tumhen pakkã mãlúm hai ?
Toom-hehn pukkah mah-loom high ?

Bring some soda water.
'Soda' le ão.
'Soda' lay aow.

Get some ice quickly.
Jaldí thorã baraf le ão.
Juldy tore-ah baraf lay aow.

Take these things away.
Ye chízen le jão.
Ye cheese-ehn lay jaow.

Put the fire out.
Ag bujhã dãlo.
Aag booj-ah dah-lo.

Burn this.
Yah jalã dãlo.
Ya julah dah-lo.

Take this chit to …
Yah chitthi …ke pãs le jão.
Ya chit-tea … kay pass lay jaow.

Bring me an answer.
Javãb le ão.
Jawaab lay aow.

Are my things ready ?
　Merí chízen taiyár hai.ı ?
　May-ree cheese-ehn tie-yar highn ?

Have you packed ?
　Tum-ne band kar lí hain ?
　Toom-nay bund kar lee highn ?

Everything ?
　Sab chízen ?
　Sub cheese-ehn ?

Forgotten nothing ?
　Kuchh bhúle to nahín ho ?
　Kootch boo-lay toe na-heehn ho ?

Bring my handbag here.
　Merí chhotí petí idhar le ão.
　May-ree cho-tea pay-tea iddar lay aow.

Fetch my stick.
　Merí lakrí le ão.
　May-ree luck-ree lay aow.

Make some sandwiches.
　Thore 'sandwich' banão.
　Tore-ray 'sandwich' bun-naow.

　　　　　Not too thick.
　　　　　Bahut mote nahín.
　　　　　Ba-hoot mow-tay na-heehn.

　　　　　You are very lazy.
　　　　　Bahut sust ho.
　　　　　Ba-hoot soost ho.

I won't stand for this.
Main yah kabhí bardãsht nahín karúngã.
Maiyn ya kab-bee burr-daasht na-heehn kar-oongah.

Don't bring your friends here.
Apne doston ko idhar mat lão.
Up-nay dostohn ko iddar mutt laow.

Tell them to get out.
Un-se kaho, ki ve chale jãen.
Oon-say kaho, key way challay ja-ehn.

You are a rascal.
Tum badmash ho.
Toom bud-maash ho.

I won't give you a reference.
Main tumhen sifãrishnãmã nahín dúngã.
Maiyn toom-hehn sifah-rish-nah-mah na-heehn doohn-gah.

I don't like your manner.
Mujhe tumhãrã dang pasand nahín.
Moojay toom-ha-rah dung pasand na-heehn.

Change your clothes.
Apne kapre badal lo.
Up-nay cup-ray bud-dull lo.

That will do (satisfied).
Voh thík hai.
Voh teak high.

Now you can go.
Ab jã sakte ho.
Ab ja suck-tay ho.

SIMPLE ORDERS : PHRASES AND QUERIES FOR EVERY DAY USAGE.

(Reminder, Pronounce "aow" as "ow" as in "cow").

Come in.
Andar ão.
Under aow.

Come later.
Bãd men ão.
Baad mayn aow.

Come Inside.
Andar ão.
Under aow.

Come before lunch.
Do-pahar ke khãne
ke pahale ão.
*Doe-pahar kay kah-
nay kay pie-lay aow.*

Look here.
Idhar dekho.
Iddar deck-o.

Too little.
Bahut kam.
Ba-hoot come.

Leave it.
Chor do.
Chore doe.

This way.
Is taraf.
Iss ta-ruff.

That way.
Us taraf.
Oos ta-ruff.

Yonder.
Udhar
Uddar.

Ask him.
Is se púchho.
Iss say pootch-o.

Thank you.
Shukriyã.
Shook-ree-ah.

Excuse me.
Mãf kijiye.
Maaf key-jee-eh.

Go away.
Chale jão.
Challay jaow.

Come here.
Idhar ão.
Iddar aow.

Come in time.
Wakt par ão.
Wakt per aow.

Come after dinner.
Khāne ke bād ão.
Kah-nay kay baad aow.

Come when it suits you.
Apni sahúliyat par ão.
Up-nee sa-hoo-lee-yat per aow.

Too much.
Bahut zyādā.
Ba-hoot zey-add-ah.

Too high.
Bahut únchā.
Ba-hoot oohn-chah.

Stay.
Thaharo.
Tie-ro.

Be careful.
Dhyān do.
Thee-aan doe.

Don't forget.
Mat bhúlo.
Mutt boo-lo.

Understand.
Samjho.
Sum-jo.

Sit down.
Baith jāo; Baitho.
Baijt-jaow; Baiyt-toe.

Stand there.
Udhar thaharo.
Uddar tie-ro.

Speak louder.
Zor se bolo.
Zore say bowl-o.

Give me.
Mujhe do.
Moojay doe.

Never mind.	**Explain.**
Fikar nahín.	Samjhão.
Ficker na-heehn.	*Sum-jaow.*
Too soon.	**Wait.**
Bahut jaldí.	Thaharo.
Ba-hoot juldy.	*Tie-ro.*
Take this.	**Later.**
Yah lo.	Bãd men.
Ya lo.	*Baad mayn.*
Don't go.	**I am sorry.**
Mat jão.	Mujhe afsos hai.
Mutt jaow.	*Moojay uf-soas high.*
Speak.	**Wait outside.**
Bolo.	Bãhar thaharo.
Bowl-o.	*Bah-her tie-ro.*
Listen.	**Wait Inside.**
Suno.	Andar thaharo.
Soon-o.	*Under tie-ro.*
Be quiet.	**Wait here.**
Chup raho.	Idhar thaharo.
Choop raho.	*Iddar tie-ro.*
Go up.	**Bring me.**
Úpar jão.	Mere liye lão.
Ooper jaow.	*May-ray lee-eh laow.*
Go down.	**Take this.**
Níche jão.	Yah lo.
Nee-chay jaow.	*Ya lo.*

Is it cold ?
Yah thandã hai kyã ?
Ya ton-dah high kay-aah ?

Put it there.
Yah udhar rakho.
Ya uddar ruck-oh.

Bring another.
Dúsrã lão.
Doos-rah laow.

Enough.
Bas; Kãfí hai.
Bus; Kah-fee high.

You are quite right.
Bilkul thík kahate ho.
Bill-cool teak ka-ha-tay ho.

Is it hot ?
Yah garam hai kyã ?
Ya gar-rum high kay-aah?

This is excellent.
Yah bahut achchhã hai.
Ya ba-hoot atch-chah high.

I said nothing.
Main kuchh nahín bolã.
Maiyn kootch na-heehn bowl-ah.

Stop.
Ruko.
Rook-o.

Bring it here.
Yah idhar lão.
Ya iddar laow.

I shall come.
Main ãúngã.
Maiyn Ah-oongah.

I am tired.
Thakã huã hún.
Tuck-ah hoo-ah hoohn.

Say I am not at home.
Bolnã ki, main ghar men nahín hún.
Bowl-nah key, maiyn ghar mayn na-heehn hoohn.

I am pleased.
Main khush hún.
Maiyn koosh hoohn.

Ring the bell.
Ghantí bajão.
Gun-tea budge-aow.

Shut the door.
Darvãzã band karo.
Der-wah-zah bund karo.

Start the fan.
Pankhã chalão.
Pung-kah chall-aow.

Call me early.
Mujhe sabere bulãnã.
Moojay sub-eh-ray bull-annah.

I am thirsty.
Mujhe pyãs lagí hai.
Moojay pea-aas lugee high.

Do what I say.
Jo kahata hun, voh karo.
Jo ka-ha-tah hoohn, voh karo.

I do not know him.
Main usè nahín jãntã.
Maiyn oosay na-heehn jaan-tah.

I am busy.
　Mujhe bahut kām hai.
　Moojay ba-hoot kaam high.

I am disappointed.
　Main nirāsh hún.
　Maiyn nee-raash hoohn.

Call the bearer.
　Baire ko bulāo.
　Bai-ray ko bull-aow.

Is anyone there ?
　Koi hai ?
　Ko-ee high ?

Open the window.
　Khirkí kholo.
　Kir-key ko-lo.

Don't wake me.
　Mujhe mat jagānā.
　Moojay mutt jug-annah.

Don't make a noise.
　Shor mat karo.
　Shore mutt karo.

I am not too well.
　Main bilkul thík nahín hún.
　Maiyn bill-cool teak na-heehn hoohn.

It sounds good.
　Yah achchhā lagtā hai.
　Ya atch-chah lug-tah high.

It sounds bad.
 Yah kharāb lagtā hai.
 Ya ka-raab lug-tah high.

Well done, indeed.
 Shābās.
 Shah-baas.

Turn him out.
 Use bāhar nikāl do.
 Oosay bah-her nick-aal doe.

Are you free ?
 Āp ko fursat hai ?
 Aap ko foor-sutt high ?

Is he here now ?
 Voh ab idhar hai ?
 Voh ab iddar high ?

I have waited a long time.
 Main bahut wakt thahara hún.
 Maiyn ba-hoot wakt tie-rah hoohn.

(Please) sit down.
 Baith jāiye.
 Baiyt ja-ee-eh.

Let him in.
 Use ander āne do.
 Oosay under ah-nay doe.

Do it today.
 Yah āj karo.
 Ya aaj karo.

Do it tomorrow.
 Yah kal karnā.
 Ya kal kar-nah.

Do it now.	**In a few days.**
Yah abhí karo.	Kuchh dinon men.
Ya a-bee karo.	*Kootch din-ohn mayn.*
In a day or two.	**Next week.**
Ek do din men.	Dúsre hafte.
Ek doe din mayn.	*Doos-ray huff-tay.*

I have an appointment.
Mujhe kisíse milnã hai.
Moojay kiss-ee-say mill-nah high.

I want to speak to him.
Main úse bolnã chãhatã hún.
Maiyn oosay bowl-nah chah-ha-tah hoohn.

Give him my card.
Use mera 'card' do.
Oosay may-rah 'card' doe.

Does he come every day.
Voh har roz ãtã hai ?
Voh her-rose ah-tah high ?

Does he stay long ?
Voh bahut thahartã hai kyã ?
Voh ba-hoot ta-her-tah high kay-aah ?

I don't understand.
Main nahíin samajhtã.
Maiyn na-heehn sum-aj-tah.

Please talk slowly.
Ãhistã boliye.
Ah-hiss-tah bowl-ee-eh.

What do you want ?
  Tumhen kyā chāhiye ?
  Toom-hehn kay-aah chah-he-eh ?

What is to be done ?
  Kyā karnā hai ?
  Kay-aah kar-nah high ?

What is your business ?
  Āp kā kaun sā vyāpār hai ?
  Aap kah cawn-sah vee-ah-par high ?

What will you eat ?
  Āp kyā khāenge ?
  Aap kay-aah kah-engay ?

What will you drink ?
  Āp kyā pienge ?
  Aap kay-aah pea-engay.

What does it mean ?
  Is kā matlab kyā hai ?
  Iss kah mut-lab kay-aah high ?

What is this ?
  Yah kyā hai ?
  Ya kay-aah high ?

What did you say ?
  Āp ne kyā kahā ?
  Aap nay kay-aah kah-ha ?

What can you do ?
  Āp kyā kar sakte hain ?
  Aap kay-aah kar suck-tay highn ?

What is it like ?
  Yah kis tarah-kā hai ?
  Ya kiss tarah-kah high ?

What do you intend to do ?
  Āp kyā karnā chāhate hain ?
  Aap kay-aah kar-nah chah-ha-tay highn ?

What is the matter ?
  Kyā bāt hai ?
  Kay-aah baat high ?

What does he do ?
  Voh kyā kartā hai ?
  Voh kay-aah kar-tah high ?

What does that mean ?
  Uskā matlab kyā hai ?
  Oos-kah mut-lub kay-aah high ?

What do you call this ?
  Ise āp kyā kahate hain ?
  Iss-ay aap kay-aah ka-ha-tay highn ?

What are you looking for ?
  Āp ko kis kā intzār hai ?
  Aap ko kiss-kah int-zaar high ?

What shall I do ?
  Kyā karūn ?
  Kay-aah karoohn ?

What does it look like ?
  Yah kis tarah dīkhtā hai ?
  Ya kiss-tarah deek-tah high ?

What price is he asking ?

Voh kitnã dãm mãngtã hai ?

Voh kit-nah daam maang-tah high ?

What is your advice ?

Ãp kí salãh kyã hai ?

Aap key salah kay-aah high ?

This is what I can offer.

Main itnã hí de saktã hún.

Maiyn itnah he they suck-tah hoohn.

I am not interested.

Yah mujhe nahín chãhiye.

Ya moojay na-heehn chah-he-eh.

I will let you know.

Tumhen batãúngã.

Toom-hehn but-ah-oohn-gah.

This is my last offer.

Main ãkhir men itnã hí dúngã.

Maiyn ah-kir mayn itnah he doohn-gah.

Tell him I called.

Us-se kahanã, ki main ne bulãyã hai.

Oos-say kah-nah, key maiyn-nay bull-ayah high.

You have been very kind.

Ãp bahut meharbãn rahe hain.

Aap bahoot may-her-baan ra-hay highn.

Shake.

Hãth Milão.

Haath Mill-aow.

Thank you all the same.
  Shukriyã.
  Shoo-kree-yah.

I shall remember you.
  Tumhen yãd karúngã.
  Toom-hehn yaad karoohn-gah.

I must take your leave.
  Ab ijãzat ho.
  Ab ija-zat ho.

I wish you all the best.
  Merí shubh kãmnãen ãp ke sãth hain.
  May-ree shoob kaam-nah-ehn aap kay saat highn.

You seem very happy.
  Ãp bahut khush díkhte hain.
  Aap bahoot koosh deek-tay highn.

You seem somewhat sad.
  Ãp kuchh udãs díkhte hain.
  Aap kootch Oodaas deek-tay highn.

I can hardly believe it.
  Main ispar wishwas nahí kar saktã.
  Maiyn iss-per wish-wass na-heehn kar suck-tah.

I am pleased to see you.
  Ãp se mil kar mujhe bahut khushí huí.
  Aap-say mill-kar moojay ba-hoot kooshee hooze.

Do not disappoint me.
  Mujhe naumed na kíjiye.
  Moojay na-oomaid na key-jee-eh.

The time is up, I am afraid.
> Mujhe dar lagtã hai, vakt ho chukã hai.
>
> *Moojay der lug-tah high, wakt ho chookah high.*

I would like to learn.
> Main síkhnã chãhúngã.
>
> *Maïyn seek-nah chah-hoohn-gah.*

Can you teach me ?
> Ãp mujhe sikhã sakte hain ?
>
> *Aap moojay sick-ah suck-tay highn ?*

Is this for sale ?
> Kyã, yah bikrí ke liye hai ?
>
> *Kay-aah ya bick-ree kay lee-eh high ?*

I received your note.
> Mujhe ãp kí chitthí milí hai.
>
> *Moojay aap key chit-tea mill-ee high.*

Sorry, I could not reply.
> Mãf karnã, main jawãb na de sakã.
>
> *Maaf kar-nah, maïyn jawaab na they suck-ah.*

I was pre-occupied.
> Main pahale hí mashgúl thã.
>
> *Maïyn pie-lay he mush-gool tah.*

It is late, I must go.
> De̐r ho gaí hai, ab mujhe jãnã chãhiye.
>
> *They-r ho ga-ee high, ab moojay ja-nah chah-he-eh.*

Do you like this climate ?
> Ãp ko idhar kí ãbo-hawã pasand hai ?
>
> *Aap ko iddar key aabo-hawah pasand high ?*

It seems to agree with you.

Aisā lagtā hai ki, yah āp ke liye achchhí hai.

Ai-sah lugtah high key, ya aap kay lee-eh atch-chee high.

Have you been here a long time ?

Āp idhar bahut wakt se hain ?

Aap iddar ba-hoot wakt say highn ?

Send for him quickly.

Uske liye jaldí bhejo.

Oos-kay lee-eh juldy bedge-o.

Or

Usko jaldí bulão.

Ooosko juldy bull-aow.

Tell him to be careful.

Use kaho, ki voh khabardār rahe.

Oos-say kaho, key voh kabar-daar ra-hay.

How many are there ?

Udhar kitne hain ?

Uddar kit-nay highn?

Don't you know ?

Kyā, tum nahín jānte ?

Kay-aah, toom na-heehn jaan-tay.

Do you understand what I said ?

Āp ne samjhā ki, main ne kyā kahā ?

Aap nay sum-jah key, maiyn nay kay-aah ka-ha?

Show me the way to the ...

... kā rāstā dikhāo.

...kah raastah dick-aow.

Give me your address.
Mujhe apnā patā do.
Moojay up-nah patah doe.

Can I have your phone number ?
Mujhe āp apnā 'phone number' denge ?
Moojay aap up-nah 'phone number' they-engay ?

I cannot find my way alone.
Main akelā apnā rāstā nachín dhúndh
sakúngā.
*Maiyn akay-lah up-nah raastah na-heehn doond
suck-oohn-gah ?*

Who are you ?
Āp kaun hain ?
Aap cawn highn ?

Who is there ?
Udhar kaun hai ?
Uddar cawn high ?

When did you arrive ?
Āp kab āe ?
Aap cub ah-eh ?

When do you leave ?
Āp kab jā rahe hain ?
Aap cub ja ra-hay highn ?

Who are these people ?
Ye log kaun hain ?
Ye log cawn highn ?

Where does he live ?
Voh kidhar rahta hai ?
Voh kiddar rah-tah high ?

Where have you been ?
Ãp kidhar the ?
Aap kiddar tay ?

Where were you yesterday?
Ãp kal kidhar the ?
Aap kal kiddar tay?

Who did this ?
Yah kisne kiyã ?
Ya kiss-nay key-aah ?

Why are you annoyed ?
Ãp nãrãz kyún hain ?
Aaap nah-raaz queon highn ?

Where do you intend to go ?
Ãp kidhar jãnã chahate hain ?
Aap kiddar ja-nah chah-ha-tay highn ?

Where did you hear this ?
Ãp ne yah kidhar sunã ?
Aap nay ya kiddar soon-ah ?

Who owns this ?
Is kã mãlik kaun hai ?
Iss kah malick cawn high ?

When is he expected ?
Voh kab ãne-wãlã hai ?
Voh cub ah-nay wallah high ?

Write it down for me.
Mere liye likh líjiye.
May-ray lee-eh lick lee-jee-eh.

Will you sign it ?
  Āp sahí karenge ?
  Aap sahee kar-engay ?

Where are you going ?
  Āp kidhar jā rahe hain ?
  Aap kiddar ja rahay highn ?

Where is my servant ?
  Merā naukar kidhar hai ?
  May-rah now-ker kiddar high ?

Where has he gone ?
  Voh kidhar gayā hai ?
  Voh kiddar gayah high ?

Who is that person ?
  Voh ādmí kaun hai ?
  Voh aadmee cawn high ?

Whose house is that ?
  Voh kiskā ghar hai ?
  Voh kiss-kah ghar high ?

Where have you come from ?
  Āp kidhar se āye hain ?
  Aap kiddar say ah-eh highn ?

Which is your native place ?
  Āp kā janam-isthān kaun-sa hai ?
  Aap kah janam-istaan cawn-sah high ?

Where can I get it ?
  Voh mujhe kidhar se milegā ?
  Voh moojay kiddar say mill-eh-gah ?

Where does that road lead to ?
Voh rāstā kidhar jātā hai ?
Voh raas-tah kiddar ja-tah high ?

SIGHTSEEING

The main objective of the tourist in India is to see the sights. And what sights there are to be seen! One can spend a thousand years in India and still not yet see all that is to be seen. As this is not a guidebook we shall content ourselves by telling the tourist that in all cities, he can travel by taxi with fixed metre rates, so there is no haggling. When long distances have to be traversed, one can make an arrangement to cover such a journey both ways, including waiting, for an agreed price. This is rather important as "waiting", may constitute many valuable hours, sometimes a whole day, when there is a range of interesting temples to be seen. An example is Belur, Halebid and Hassan. Here there are many temples all within walking distance of each other. To see them properly one requires one or two whole days at the least. In such cases hiring a car for the whole day is the best arrangement. The Tourist Department runs a series of char-à-bancs to such well known places and it is for the tourist to decide whether he prefers to go in a party or on his own.

Outside the cities, journeys may have to be made by tonga - pony cart. As a diversion, this always makes for an interesting trip apart from the considerable "shakeup" that one may experience on bad roads. The rates for trips by such pony carts are very low, certainly not exceeding a few modest rupees for one whole day. In some places (somewhat rarely, thank goodness) stages of the journey may have to be completed by bullock cart. Except to say that "slow but sure is the only way" further comment would be superfluous.

What is to be seen here?
 Idhar kyā dekhne läik hai ?
 Iddar kay-aah deck-nay lah-ick high ?

How many temples are there ?
 Idhar kitne mandir hain ?
 Iddar kit-nay mandir highn ?

Are the ruins near ?
 Khandhar naz-dik hain ?
 Kand-her naz-deek highn ?

Where is the fort ?
 Kilā kidhar hai ?
 Kill-ah kiddar high ?

How does one get there ?
 Udhar kis taraf se jānā hoga ?
 Uddar kiss ta-ruff say ja-nah hogah ?

Is there a church nearby ?
 Idhar koí 'church' nazdík hai ?
 Iddar ko-ee 'church' naz-deek high ?

I want to see the cemetery.
 Main makbarā dekhnā chāhatā hún.
 Maiyn muck-barah deck-nah chah-ha-tah hoohn.

Please direct me there.
 Mujhe udhar le chaliye.
 Moojay uddar lay chall-ee-eh.

Can you get me a guide ?
 Āp mujhay rāstā dikhāne-waiā le denge ?
 Aap moojay raastah dick-ah-nay wallah lay they-engay ?

What does he charge ?
 Voh kitne paise lata hai ?
 Voh kitnay pice-eh lay-tay high ?

Can we go by taxi ?
 Ham 'taxi' se jā sakte hain ?
 Hum 'taxi' say jā sucktay highn ?

Is a bullock cart comfortable ?
Kyā ham bail-gārí men ārām se jā sakte hain?
Kay-aah hum bale-gaaree mayn aaraam say ja suck-tay highn ?

Is the museum worth seeing ?
Ajāyab-ghar dekhne lāik hai ?
Ajah-yab-ghar deck-nay lah-ick high ?

Can we get into the palace ?
Hum mahal men jā sakte hain ?
Hum mahal mayn ja suck-tay highn ?

What time does it open ?
Yah kitne baje khultā hai ?
Ya kit-nay budg-eh cool-tah high ?

Is it open today ?
Voh āj khulā hai kyā?
Voh aaj cool-ah high kay-aah ?

Is it open everyday ?
Voh har-roz khulā rahtā hai ?
Voh her-rose cool-ah rah-tah high ?

What is the admission ?
Dākhilā-fee kitní hai ?
Dak-lah-fee kit-nee high ?

What are the hours ?
Khulne kā wakt kyā hai ?
Cool-nay kah wakt kay-aah high ?

How old is this?
Yah kitnā purānā hai ?
Ya kit-nah poorah-nah high?

What is its history ?
　Is kã ithiãs kyã hai ?
　Isskah it-haas kay-aah high ?

How long did it take ?
　Iske banne men kitnã wakt lagã ?
　Isskay bun-nay mayn kit-nah wakt lugah ?

Must we make written application ?
　Kyã hamko likh kar arzí dení hogí ?
　Kay-aah hum-ko lick-kar arzee they-nee hogee ?

Are there cottage industries here ?
　Idhar gharelú hunar hote hai ?
　Iddar gharay-loo hoonar ho-tay highn ?

Where are they ?
　Ve kidhar hain ?
　Way kiddar highn ?

And handicrafts ?
　Aur dast-kãrí ? (Hãth se bani chízen).
　Owr dust-car-ee ? (Haath say bunny cheese-ehn)

Can we take photograps ?
　Hum 'photo' khínch sakte hain ?
　Hum 'photo' keench suck-tay highn ?

Are there any good paintings ?
　Udhar achche chitra hain ?
　Uddar atch-chay chit-ra highn ?

Do we take our shoes off ?
　Hamko apne júte utãrne chãhiye kyã ?
　Humko up-nay jootay ootaar-nay chah-he-eh kay-aah ?

Can we wear hats inside ?

Ham top pahan kar andar jã sakte hain ?

Hum tope pahan kar under ja suck-tay highn ?

Can we have a guide-book ?

Hamko rãstã batãne walí kitãb mil saktí hai?

Humko raastah but-ah-nay wallee kitaab mill suck-tea high ?

What does it cost?

Uskí kímat kyã hai ?

Oos-key key-mutt kay-aah high ?

Can we go in a party ?

Ham sab sãth men jã sakte hain ?

Hum sub saath mayn ja suck-tay highn ?

Can we have an interpreter ?

Hamko idhar koi samjhãne wãlã mill saktã hai ?

Humko iddar ko-ee sum-ja-nay-wallah mill suck-tah high ?

Tell him to speak slowly.

Use kaho, ki ãhistã bole.

Oossay ka-ho, key ah-hiss-tah bowl-eh.

He talks too fast.

Voh bahut tez boltã hai.

Voh bahoot taize bowl-ta high.

Ask him to speak louder.

Use kaho, ki zorse bole.

Oos-say kaho key zore-say bowl-eh.

Do tourists get special facilities ?
Sailaniyon ke liye khas sahúliyaten hain
kyã ?
*Sailanee-ohn kay lee-eh kaas sahoo-lee-at-ehn
highn kay-aah ?*

Can we watch the ceremony ?
Ham pújã dekh sakte hain ?
Hum poojah deck suck-tay highn ?

Are there sacred rivers near ?
Koí pawitra nadiyãn nazdik hain ?
Ko-ee pa-wit-ra nadee-yahn naz-deek highn ?

Can we photograph the priests?
Ham purohiton ke 'photo' khinch sakte hain ?
*Hum poora-hit-ohn kay 'photo' keench sucktay
highn ?*

We want to see temple cars.
Ham mandiron ke rath dekhnã chãhate hain.
*Hum mandeer-ohn kay rath deck-nah chah-ha-tay
highn.*

When is the next festival ?
Dúsrã tyohãr kab hai ?
Doos-rah tee-yo-haar cub high ?

How do we get back ?
Ham kis tarah wãpas jã sakenge ?
Hum kiss tarah wah-pus ja suck-engay ?

Is there any place to eat ?
Khãne ke liye koí jagah hai ?
Kah-nay kay lee-eh ko-ee jug-ah high ?

Is it safe to go there ?
 Udhar jãne men salāmati hai ?
 Uddar ja-nay mayn salah-mattee high ?

What is the best ti.ne to go there ?
 Udhar jãne ke liye, sab se achchhã kaun
 sã wakt hai ?
 *Uddar ja-nay kay lez-eh, subsay atch-chah cawn-
 sah wakt high ?*

Must we leave so early ?
 Itnā sabere jānā zarurí hai kyā ?
 It-nah sub-eh-ray ja-nah zarooree high kay-aah ?

Does the hotel give us sandwiches ?
 Ham ko 'Hotel' men 'sandwich' mil sakenge?
 Humko 'hotel' mayn 'sandwich' mill suck-engay?

Can we get a packed lunch basket ?
 Hum ko dopahar kã khānā band kar de
 sakte hain ?
 *Hum ko doe-pahar kah kah-nah bund kar they
 suck-tay highn ?*

Is there a good zoo here ?
 Idhar achchhã chiriyã-ghar hai ?
 Iddar atch-chah chiree-yah-ghar high ?

What sort of animals does one see ?
 Kaun kaun se jãnwar udhar dekhne ko
 milenge ?
 *Cawn cawn say jaan-ver udder deck-nay ko mill-
 engay ?*

Is there an aquarium ?
Udhar machhlí-ghar hai ?
Uddar much-lee-gar high ?

Is it worth seeing ?
Voh dekhne lãik hai ?
Voh deck-nay lah-ick high ?

Any crocodiles about ?
Idhar magarmachh bhí hain ?
Iddar ma-ger-much bee highn ?

Can we see them ?
Ham unko dekh sakte hain ?
Hum oon-ko deck suck-tay highn ?

What about snakes ?
Aur sãnp ?
Owr saahnp ?

Many about ?
Bahut hain kyã ?
Ba-hoot highn kay-aah ?

And elephants ?
Aur hãthí ?
Owr ha-tee ?

Can we ride on them ?
Ham unpar sawãrí kar sakte hain ?
Hum oon-per savah-ree kar suck-tay highn ?

See them bathe ?
Unko ghusal karte wakt dekh sakte hain ?
Oon-ko goosal kar-tay wakt deck suck-tay highn?

Can you suggest a programme ?
Ãp kārya-kram batā sakte hain ?
Aap car-yah-crum batah suck-tay highn ?

How long would it take ?
Is men kitnā wakt lagegā ?
Iss mayn kit-nah wakt lug-eh-gah ?

Is it worthwhile ?
Kyā yah thík hai ?
Kay-aah ya teak high ?

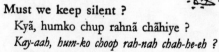

Can we speak here ?
Ham idhar bol sakte hain ?
Hum iddar bowl suck-tay highn ?

Must we keep silent ?
Kyā, humko chup rahnā chāhiye ?
Kay-aah, hum-ko choop rah-nah chah-he-eh ?

Can we touch this ?
Ham isko hāth lagā sakte hain ?
Hum issko haat lugah suck-tay highn ?

Is he annoyed ?
Voh nārāz hai kyā ?
Voh nah-raaz high kay-aah ?

Now we must go.
 Ab hamko jānā chāhiye.
 Ab humko ja-nah chah-he-eh.

Take us back.
 Hamko wāpus le chalo.
 Humko wah-pus lay challo.

SHOPPING

Shopping in India can be an intriguing experience. Unlike many Eastern countries and Aden where shopkeepers start off with a price about five times in excess of what they expect ultimately to get, there are bazaar dealers in India who follow the same principle but not quite to the same extent. Approximately double what they expect to get in the end is the starting-off price. Thereafter it is a battle of wits, usually conducted in the highest of spirits, loud voices and the most expressive of gesticulations, but none the less in a friendly atmosphere. It is all part of the game. In all the larger cities and most certainly in all Government sponsored enterprises such as the Cottage Industries Emporiums, Handloom Houses etc., prices are fixed and there is no haggling as nearly all articles for sale carry a price tag affixed. To buy is both exciting and illuminating. Take carpets, silks, and brocades, for instance. An attendant will unroll bales of priceless silk before your eyes until you cannot think straight. He will unroll endless stocks of carpets from Kashmir, Persia, and all out-of-the-world places. Some pure silk, some woollen and some coir. It depends upon what you are interested in. Then he will leave you to think and while you are thinking he will offer you a cold drink or a hot coffee. And if you don't buy he will not be disconsolate. He will be a model of old world courtesy, show you to the exit and plead for you to come again. It is this "magic" personality that seems to draw the customer back again, not once but many times.

We want to see the shops.
Ham dúkãnen dekhnã chãhate hain.
Hum dookaan-ehn deck-nah cha-ha-tay highn.

Is the bazaar the best place?
Bãzãr achchhã hai ?
Bazaar atch-chah high ?

Take us there.
Hamko udhar le challo.
Humko uddar lay chalo.

I am going into this shop.

Main is dúkān men jãtā hún.

Maiyn iss dookaan mayn ja-tah hoohn.

I want to buy jewellery.

Main zewar kharídnā chāhatā hún.

Maiyn zay-wer kareed-nah chah-ha-tah hoohn.

I am interested in bracelets, rings, stones, necklaces, earrings, handbags, perfumes, skins, furs.

Main kangan, angúthiyãã, jawãher, hãr, kãnke zewar, chhote-bag, itra, khãlen, aur pashmí khãlen dekhnā chāhatā hún.

Maiyn kungan, angoo-tea-yahn, jawah-her, haar, kaan kay zay-wer, chotay bag , attar, call-ehn, owr pashme call-ehn deck-nah cha-ha-tah hoohn.

What is the price of this ?

Iskã dãm kyã hai ?

Isskah daam kay-aah high ?

It is too much.

Yah bahut zyãdã hai.

Ya ba-hoot zey-add-ah high.

What is your last price ?

Ãkhír kyã dãm loge ?

Ah-kir kay-aah daam lo-gay?

I haven't got so much.

Mere pas itne paise nahín hain.

May-ray pass it-nay pice-eh na-heehn highn.

I will give you ....
>Main ..dúngã.
>*Maiyn .. doohn-gah.*

It is too dear.
>Yah bahut mahangã hai.
>*Ya ba-hoot ma-hengah high.*

What will you take for this ?
>Iskã kitnã loge ?
>*Iss-kah kit-nah lo-gay.*

Show me a sample.
>Mujhe namúna dikhão.
>*Moojay na-moon-ah dick-aow.*

Let me have my bill.
>Mujhe 'bill' do.
>*Moojay 'bill' doe.*

Count the money.
>Paise gino.
>*Pice-eh gean-oh.*

Give me my change.
>Bãki rezgí wãpas do.
>*Bah-key rays-gee wah-pus doe.*

This bill is not correct.
>Yah 'bill' thík nahín hai.
>*Ya 'bill' teak na-heehn high.*

Show me a better quality.
>Is se bhí achchhí chíz dikhão.
>*Iss say bee atch-chee cheese dick-aow.*

I want only good articles.
Mujhay sirf achchhí chízen chāhiye.
Moojay sirf atch-chee cheese-ehn chah-he-eh.

Is this your best ?
Tumhāre pãs sabse achchhí yahí chíz hai ?
Toom-ha-ray pass sub-say atch-chee ya-he cheese high?

It is not what I want.
Yah voh chíz nahín, jo moojay chahiye.
Ya voh cheese na-heehn, jo moojay chah-he-eh.

This will do.
Yah thík hai.
Ya teak high.

This is just the same.
Yah to us jaisí hí hai.
Ya toe oos jai-see he high.

Please wrap them up.
Ye band kíjiye.
Ye bund key-jee-eh.

Do I get a discount ?
Mujhe Katauti milegí ?
Moojay cutow-tee mill-eh-gee ?

Is this quite new ?
Yah bilkul nayã hai kyã ?
Ya bill-cool nayah high kay-aah ?

Will you give a guarantee ?
Tum 'guarantee' doge ?
Toom 'guarantee' doe-gay ?

Will you deliver it to my hotel ?

Āp, yah mere 'hotel' men bhej denge ?

Aap, ya may-ray 'hotel' mayn bedge they-engay ?

What do you charge for delivery ?

Bhej-ne ke kitne paise lete hain ?

Bedge-nay kay kit-nay pice-eh laytay highn ?

Can you post it for me ?

Āp mere liye dāk zariye bhej denge ?

Aap may-ray lee-eh 'dak' zaree-eh bedge they-engay?

Can I rely on you ?

Main tum par wishwās rakhún ?

Maiyn toom per wish-wass ruck-hoohn ?

Is the colour fast ?

Yah rang pakkā hai ?

Ya rung pakkah high ?

I want nothing else.

Mujhe aur kuchh nahín chāhiye.

Moojay owr kootch na-heehn chah-he-eh.

This does not fit.

Yah thík nahín hai.

Ya teak na-heehn high.

It is faded.

Iskā rang phíkā ho gayā hai.

Iss-kah rung pheak-ah ho gayah high.

Are not your prices fixed ?

Tumhāre dām mukarrar nahín kyā ?

Toom-ha-ray daam mookar-er na-heehn kay-aah ?

Have you not another kind ?

Tumhāre pās dúsrā namúnā nahín kyã ?

Toom-ha-ray pass doos-rah na-moon-ah na-heehn kay-aah ?

Show it to me.

Mujhe dikhão.

Moojay dick-aow.

This looks very old.

Yah bahut purãnā díkhtā hai.

Ya bahoot poorah-nah dick-tah high.

It has been badly handled.

Yah thík tarah nahín rakhã gayã.

Ya teak tarah na-heehn ruck-ah gayah.

How much is this per metre ?

Iske ek 'meter' kã kyã dãm hai ?

Iss-kay ek 'meter' kah kay-aah daam high ?

Give me an extra piece.

Mujhe zyãdã tukrã do.

Moojay zey-add-ah took-rah doe.

I like this one.

Mujhe yah chãhiye.

Moojay ya chah-he-eh.

I do not like that one.

Mujhe voh nahín chãhiye.

Moojay voh na-heehn chah-he-eh.

I want it in blue.

Yah níle rang kã do.

Ya neelay rung kah doe.

You call this a bargain ?

Kyã ise mol-tol ka-ha-tay ho ?

Kay-aah issay mole-toll ka-ha-tay ho ?

It is too expensive.

Yah bahut mahaingã hai.

Ya ba-hoot ma-heng-ah high.

Give me a reduction.

Iske dãm men kuchh kam karo.

Iss-kay daam mayn kootch kam karo.

I shall take it with me.

Yah apne sãth le jãúngã.

Ya up-nay saat lay ja-oohn-gah.

Have you got scarves ?

Tumhãre pas bare rúmãl hain ?

Toom-ha-ray pass burray roo-maal high ?

I am just having a look around.

Main sirf dekhne ãyã hún.

Maiyn sirf deck-nay ayah hoohn.

I do not like the style.

Yah namúna mujhe pasand nahín.

Ya na-moon-ah moojay pasand na-heehn.

It doesn't suit me.

Yah mujhay thík nahín lagtã.

Ya moojay teak na-heehn lug-tah.

I want a blouse.

Mujhay 'blouse' chãhiye.

Moojay 'blouse' chah-he-eh.

Show me what you have.

Jo tumhãre pãs hai, voh dikhão.

Jo toom-ha-ray pass high, voh dick-aow.

Nothing in nylon ?

'Nylon' kã nahín kyã ?

'Nylon' kah na-heehn kay-aah ?

Or in pure silk ?

Yã resham kã ?

Ya ray-shum kah ?

Have you brocades ?

Tumhãre pãs kimkhãb ke kapre hain ?

Toom-ha-ray pass kim-kaab kay cup-ray highn ?

Let me see them.

Ve Mujhay dikhão.

Way Moojay dick-aow.

Is this handsewn ?

Yah hãth se siyã huã hai ?

Ya haat say see-ah hoo-ah high ?

It is not hand work.

Yah dastkãrí nahín. (Yah hãth kã kãm nahín).

Ya dust-car-ee na-heehn. (Ya haat kah kaam na-heehn).

Is this made locally ?

Yah idhar ke logon ne banãyã hai ?

Ya iddar kay lo-gohn nay bun-ayah high ?

Have you anything imported ?

Tumhãre pãs koí videshí chízen haín ?

Toom-ha-ray pass ko-ee vi-they-she cheese-ehn highn?

The sleeves are too long.
Ãstínen bahut lambí hain.
Aasteen-ehn ba-hoot lumbee highn ?

The sleeves are too short.
Ãstínen bahut chhotí hain.
Aasteen-ehn ba-hoot chotee highn.

It should be narrower.
Yah aur bhí chhotã honã chãhiye.
Ya owr bee chotah honah chah-he-eh.

It should be wider.
Yah aur bhí chaurã honã chãhiye.
Yah owr bee chow-rah honah chah he-eh.

I want it shorter.
Yah mujhe aur bhí chotã chãhiye.
Ya moojay owr bee chotah chah-he-eh.

May I try this one ?
Yah azmã kar dekhún ?
Ya aaz-mah kar deck-hoohn ?

Show me some perfumes.
Mujhe itar dikhão.
Moojay attar dick-aow.

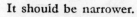

Is this bag hand-made.
Yah 'bag' hãth kí baní huí hai ?
Ya 'bag' haat key bunee hoo-ee high ?

I shall come back again.
Main phir ãúngã.
Maiyn fear ah-oohn-gah.

When I have more time.
Jab mujhe zyādā wakt hogā.
Jub moojay zey-add-ah wakt ho-gah.

I will return later.
Main bād men āúngā.
Maiyn baad mayn ah-oohn-gah.

Can you show me something else ?
Aur kuchh dikhā sakte ho ?
Our kootch dick-ah suck-tay ho ?

This looks beautiful.
Yah sundar lagtā hai.
Ya soon-der lugtah high.

This feels wonderful.
Wāh, kamāl hai.
Wah, kamaal high.

You think I am a millionaire ?
Tum samajhte ho ki, main lakhpatí hún ?
Toom sum-aj-tay ho key, maiyn luck-patee hoohn?

EVERYDAY CLOTHING

Aprons.
Pesh band.
Paysh bund.

Cape.
Garebãn.
Garay-baan.

Bands.
Pattiyãn.
Putt-tee-ahn.

Chemise.
Kamíz.
Kameez.

Bathrobe.
Nahãne kí poshãk.
Na-ha-nay key po-shaak.

Clothes.
Kapre.
Cup-ray.

Bodice.
Cholí.
Cholee.

Coat.
Kot.
Coat.

Blanket.
Kambal.
Come-bal.

Collar.
Collar.
Collar.

Blouse.
Blouse.
Blouse.

Corset.
Angiyã.
Ung-ee-ah.

Brassiers.
Brassiers.
Brassiers.

Curtains.
Parde.
Purday.

Cap.
Topí.
Tow-pee.

Drawers.
Pãjãmã.
Paajaamah.

Dress.
Poshāk.
Po-shaak.

Dressing-gown.
Dressing-poshāk.
Dressing-po-shaak.

Embroidery.
Zar-dozí.
Zar-dozee.

Frock.
Frock.
Frock.

Handkerchief.
Rúmāl.
Roo-maal.

Napkin.
Chhotā Tauliyā.
Chotah Tow-lee-ah.

Night dress.
Rāt kí poshāk.
Raat key po-shaak.

Nylon.
Nylon.
Nylon.

Petticoat.
Ghāgrā.
Gah-grah.

Pillow.
Takiyā.
Tuck-ee-yah.

Pullover.
Jarúsí.
Jaroosee.

Pyjamas.
Pājāmā.
Paajaamah.

Rain Coat.
Barsāt́ coat.
Bursah-tee coat.

Scarf.
Barā rúmāl.
Burrah roo-maal.

Shirt.
Kamíz.
Kameez.

Sheet.
Chādar.
Chah-der.

Shorts.
Nekar.
Knicker.

Silk.
Resham.
Rayshum.

Slip.
Petticoat.
Petticoat.

Socks.
Moze.
Mozay.

Stockings.
Moze.
Mozay.

Suspenders.
Suspenders;
Braces.
Suspenders ; Braces.

Sweater.
Sweater.
Sweater.

Ties.
Ties.
Ties.

Towel.
Tauliyã.
Tow-lee-ah.

Trousers.
Patlún.
Patloon.

Turban.
Pagrí.
Pugree.

Underpants.
Jhãngiyã.
Jaangee-ah.

Undervest.
Baniãn.
Bunny-aan.

MEASUREMENTS

Length.
Lambãí.
Lumb-ah-ee.

Small.
Chhotã.
Chotah

High.
Unchã.
Oonchah.

Long.
Lambã.
Lumb-ah.

Thin.
Patlã.
Patlah.

Narrow.
Tang.
Tongue.

New.
Nayã.
Nayah.

Newer.
Zyãdã nayã.
Zey-add-ah nayah.

Width.
Chaurãí.
Chow-rah-ee.

Large.
Barã.
Burrah.

Low.
Níche.
Neechay.

Short.
Chhotã.
Chotah.

Thick.
Motã.
Moat-ah.

Wide.
Chaurã.
Chow-rah.

Old.
Purãnã.
Poor-ah-nah.

Older.
Zyãdã purãnã.
Zey-add-ah poorahnah.

Smaller.
Zyãdã chhotã.
Zey-add-ah chotah.

Higher.
Zyãdã Unchã.
Zey-add-ah oonchah.

Longer.	**Lower.**
Zyādā lambā.	Zyādā níche.
Zey-add-ah lumb-ah.	*Zey-add-ah neechay.*
Thinner.	**Shorter.**
Zyādā patlā.	Zyādā chhotā.
Zey-add-ah patlah.	*Zey-add-ah chotah.*
Narrower.	**Thicker.**
Zyādā tang.	Zyādā motā.
Zey-add-ah tongue.	*Zey-add-ah moat-ah.*
Larger.	**Wider.**
Zyādā barā.	Zyādā chaurā.
Zey-add-ah burrah.	*Zey-add-ah chow-rah.*

Height.
Unchāí.
Oonchah-ee.

COLOURS

Black.
Kālā
Kaalah

Green.
Harā
Harah

Blue.
Nílā
Neelah

Grey.
Kabútarí
Kaboo-taree rung

Brown.
Bhúrā
Boorah

Light.
Halkā
Hal-kah

Colour.
Rang
Rang

Orange.
Nārangí rang
Nah-rungee rung

Dark.
Kālā
Kaalah

Purple.
Jāmuní
Jamoonee

Red.
Lāl
Laal

White.
Safed
Safeyd

Violet.
Bainganí
Bang-anee

Yellow.
Pílā
Peelah

NAMES OF COMMON SHOPS

Bookshop.
Kitāb-ghar.
Kitaab-gar.

Clothier.
Bajāj; Kapre-wālā.
*Budge-aj; Cup-ray
wallah.*

Chemist.
Dawā-farosh.
Dawah-furosh.

Fruitshop.
Mewe kí dúkān.
*May-way key doo-
kaan.*

Hats.
Top.
Tope.

Market.
Mărket, Bāzăr.
·Market, Bazaar.

Shoe.
Jútā.
Jootah.

Dressmaker.
Darzí.
Darzee.

Florist.
Phúl-wālā.
Fool-wallah.

Hardware.
Lohe kā sāmān.
*Low-hay kah saa-
maan.*

Jewellery.
Zewarāt.
Zaywar-aat.

Music shop.
Sangít ke sāzon kí
dúkān.
*Sun-geet kay saaz-
ohn key dookaan.*

Tailor.
Darzí.
Darzee.

Watchmaker.
Gharí-sāz.
Gur-ree-saaz.

Toys.
Khilaune.
Kill-own-eh.

Tobacconist.
Tambākú-wālā.
Tambaakoo-wallah.

Optician.
Chashme-wālā.
Chashmay-wallah..

Curios.
Nirālí kalāpúran chízen.
Nirah-lee kalah-pooran cheese-ehn.

TRAVEL BY TRAIN

Call a taxi.
  'Taxi' bulāo.
  'Taxi' bull-aow.
Call a carriage.
  Gãdí bulāo.
  Gar-ree bull-aow.
Where is the station ?
  'Station' kidhar hai ?
  'Station' kidder high ?
How far is it to the station ?
  Voh 'station' se kitnã dúr hai ?
  Voh 'station' say kitnah doo-r high ?
Where is the ticket office ?
  'Ticket office' kidhar hai ?
  'Ticket office' kidder high ?

I want a ticket to New Delhi.
Mujhe 'New Delhi' kā 'ticket' chāhiye.
Moojay 'New Delhi' kah 'ticket' chah-he-eh.

First class.
Pahalā darjā.
Pie-lah der-ja.

Second class.
Dúsrā darjā.
Doos-rah der-ja.

Single.
Sirf jāne kā.
Sirf ja-nay kah.

Return.
Jāne āne kā.
Ja-nay ah-nay kah.

How much does it cost?
Kitne paise lagte hain?
Kit-nay pice-eh lug-tay highn?

Has the train sleeping accommodation?
Rel-gāri men sone kā bandobast hai?
Rail-gar-ee mayn so-nay kah bundo-bust high?

Is it air-conditioned?
Voh 'air-conditioned' hai?
Voh 'air-conditioned' high?

Is bedding provided?
Bister miltā hai?
Bis-ter mill-tah high?

Is it a slow train?
Voh dhímí gārí hai?
Voh deem-ee gar-ree high?

Is it a fast train ?

Voh tez gãrí hai ?

Voh taize gar-ee high ?

Can I register my baggage ?

Main apnã sãmãn 'register' karã saktã hún ?

Maiyn up-nah saamaan 'register' kar-ah suck-tah hoohn ?

That is my luggage there.

Voh merã sãmãn hai.

Voh may-rah saamaan high.

These are my bags too.

Yah sãmãn bhi merã hai .

Ya saamaan bee may-rah high.

Put them in the compartment.

Ye sab dabbe me rakho.

Ye sub dub-bay mayn ruck-oh.

When does the train arrive ?

Rel-gãrí kitne baje ãtí hai ?

Rail-gar-ree kit-nay budge-eh ah-tea high ?

When does the train leave ?

Rel-gãrí kitne baje jãtí hai ?

Rail-gar-ree kit-nay budge-eh ja-tee high ?

How long is the journey ?

Musãfirí kitní lambí hai ?

Moosah-free kit-nee lumb-ee high ?

Do we stop at all stations ?

Kyã, ham har-ek 'station' par rukte hain ?

Kay-aah hum her-ek 'station' per rook-tay highn?

Is there a dining-car attached ?
  Rel-gã í men khãne kã dabbã hai ?
  Rail-gar-ree mayn kah-nay kah dub-bah high ?

Where is it on the train ?
  Rel-gãrí men voh kis taraf hai ?
  Rail-gar-ree mayn voh kiss ta-ruff high ?

Can one get food at the stations ?
  'Station'-on par khãnã miltã hai ?
  'Station'-ohn per kah-nah mill-tah high ?

Is the drinking water reliable ?
  Yah pãní píne lãik hai ?
  Ya paanee pea-nay lah-ick high ?

Has it been boiled ?
  Yah ubãlã gayã hai ?
  Ya oo-ball-ah gayah high ?

Is milk too always boiled?
  Dúdh bhí hameshã garam kiyã jãtã hai ?
  Dood bee hum-eh-shah gar-rum key-aah ja-tah high?

Bring me soda-water.
  'Soda-water' le ão.
  'Soda-water' lay aow.

It is terribly dusty here.
  Idhar bahut mittí hai.
  Iddar ba-hoot mit-tea high.

Please have the compartment cleaned.
  Rel kã dabbã sãf karãíye.
  Rail kah dub-bah saaf karah-ee-eh.

Open the windows.
   Khirkiyãn kholo.
   Kir-key-ahn kolo.

Pull the shutters down.
   'Shutter' níche karo.
   'Shutter' neechay karo.

Can you smoke in here ?
   Tum idhar tambākú pí sakte ho ?
   Toom iddar tambaakoo pea suck-tay ho ?

This bathroom is filthy.
   Yah pākhānā bahut gandā hai.
   Ya pah-kaanah ba-hoot gun-dah high.

Have it washed at once.
   Yah jaldí sāf karāo.
   Ya juldy saaf kar-aow.

The fans are not working.
   Pankhe nahín chalte hain.
   Punkay na-heehn chall-tay highn.

Inform the guard immediately.
   'Guard' ko jaldí batāo.
   'Guard' ko juldy but-aow.

Can I get a newspaper here ?
   Mujhe idhar akhbār mil sakegā ?
   Moojay iddar ak-bar mill suck-eh-gah ?

There is no running water either.
   Nalke men pāní bhí nahín hai.
   Null-kay mayn paanee bee na-heehn high.

Tell the guard when he comes.

Jab 'guard' āe, to usko batānā.

Jub 'guard' ah-eh, toe oos-ko but-annah.

Are we leaving late ?

Ham der se jā rahe hain kyā ?

Hum they-r say ja rahay highn kay-aah ?

Why doesn't it start ?

Yah abhí tak chati kyún nahín ?

Ya a-bee tuck chall-tea queon na-heehn ?

How long do we stop at stations ?

Ham 'station'-on par kitní der tak rukte hain?

Hum 'station'-ohn per kit-nee they-r tuck rook-tay highn ?

Lower the top seat.

Upar wālí 'seat' níche karo.

Oo-per waallee 'seat' nee-chay karo.

Spread my bedding out.

Mera bister lagāo.

May-rah bis-ter lug-aow.

When shall we get there ?

Ham udhar kab pahunchenge.

Hum uddar cub pa-hoohnch-engay.

Get a hand fan from somewhere.

Kahín se pankhā le āo.

Kaheehn say punkah lay aow.

It is unbearably hot.

Garmí sahane ke bāhar hai.

Gar-me sa-ha-nay kay bah-her high.

Bring some cake and tea.
> Kuchh 'cake' aur chāy le āo.
> *Kootch 'cake' owr chah lay aow.*

Wake me at down.
> Mujhay prabhāt ko jagānā.
> *Moojay pra-baat ko jug-annah.*

Call a porter.
> 'Coolie' ko bulāo.
> *'Coolie' ko bull-aow.*

Give him these baggage tickets.
> Sāmān ke 'ticket' usko do.
> *Saamaan kay 'ticket' oos-ko doe.*

See that the luggage is correct.
> Dekho ki sāmān thík hai.
> *Deck-o key saamaan teak high.*

Call a taxi or horse carriage.
> 'Taxi' yā ghorā-gāṛí bulāo.
> *Taxi' yah gorah-gar-ree bull-aow.*

How much is the fare ?
> Kitnā kirāyā hai ?
> *Kit-nah kirah-yah high ?*

That is far too much.
> Yah bahut zyādā hai.
> *Ya ba-hoot zey-add-ah high.*

I shall give you...
> Main tumhen ...dúngā.
> *Maiyn toom-hehn...doohn-gah.*

I want a window seat.

Mujhe khirkí ke nazdík walí jagah chāhiye.

Moojay kir-key kay naz-deek wallee jug-ah chah-he-eh.

Can I get a time table ?

Mujhe 'time table' mil sakega ?

Moojay 'time table' mill suck-eh-gah ?

I want to send this luggage.

Main yah sāmān bhejnā chāhatā hùn,

Maiyn ya saamaan bedge-nah chah-ha-tah hoohn.

I wish to insure my luggage.

Main apne sāmān kā bìmā karānā chāhāta hùn.

Maiyn up-nay saaman kah bee-mah Karah-nah Chah-ha-tah hoohn.

Here is the ticket.

Yeh merā 'ticket' hai.

Ya may-rah 'ticket' high.

Can I have an upper berth ?

Mujhe úpar wālí sone kí jagah mil sakegí ?

Moojay ooper-wallee so-nay key jug-ah mill suck-eh-gee ?

Get some ice as well.

Kuchh baraf bhí le āo.

Kootch ba-ruff bee lay aow.

Put the luggage in the van.

Gārí men sāmān rakho.

Gar-ree mayn saamaan ruck-oh.

TRAVEL BY AIR

Whereabout is the air-port ?
  Hawãí-addã kis taraf hai ?
  Ha-wah-ee-addah kiss-ta-ruff high ?

How long does it take to get there ?
  Udhar pahunchne men kitnã wakt lagtã hai?
  Uddar pa-hoohnch-ney mayn kit-nah wakt lug-tah high ?

Is there a regular bus-service ?
  Udhar 'but' bãkãyadã jatí hai ?
  Uddar 'bus' bah-kah-yadah ja-tea high ?

Will it pick me up on the way ?
  Rãste men, main usmen charh saktã hún ?
  Raastay mayn, maiyn oos-mayn char suck-tah hoohn?

When is there a flight to Mumbai ?

   'Mumbai' ko hawāī-jahāz kab jāegā ?

   'Mumbai' ko ha-wah-ee ja-haaz cub ja-eh-gah ?

Can you book me seats for .... ?

   ...jāne ke liye, āp merī 'seats' rakh sakte hain?

   ...ja-nay kay lee-eh, aap may-ree 'seats' ruck suck-tay highn ?

What is the flight number ?

   Hawai-jahāz kā 'number' kyā hai ?

   Ha-wah-ee-ja-haaz kah 'number' kay-aah high ?

At what time does it leave ?

   Voh kitne baje jātā hai ?

   Voh kit-nay budge-eh ja-tah high ?

In case of cancellation, what happens ?

   Radd karne kī hālat men kyā hotā hai ?

   Rud kar-nay key ha-lut mayn kay-aah hotah high?

How many kilos may I take ?

   Main kitne 'kilo' le jā saktā hún ?

   Maiyn kit-nay 'kilo' lay ja suck-tah hoohn ?

What is the excess charge ?

   Zyādā sāmān ke kitne paise ?

   Zey-add-ah saamaan kay kitnay pice-eh ?

TRAVEL BY SEA

When does the ship sail ?
  Jahāz kab jātā hai ?
  Ja-haaz cub ja-tah high ?

What ship is it ?
  Voh kaun-sā jahāz hai ?
  Voh cawn-sah ja-haaz high ?

Is there a boat to Cochin ?
  Cochin ke liye nāw hai kyā ?
  Cochin kay lee-eh naow high kay-aah ?

How often does it sail ?
  Voh kitnī bār jāti hai ?
  Voh kit-nee bar ja-tea high ?

How many times a day ?
  Din men kitnī bār ?
  Din mayn kit-nee bar ?

Has my luggage gone on board ?
Merā sāmān jahāz men rakhā gayā hai ?
May-rah saamaan jahaaz mayn ruck-ah gayah high?

Hire a boat.
Nāw kirāye par lo.
Naow kirah-eh per lo.

Hire a lanch.
'Launch' kirāye par lo.
'Launch' kirah-eh per lo.

Is there a berth vacant ?
Jahāz men 'berth' khalī hai ?
Jahaaz mayn 'berth' call-ee high ?

Where can I get tickets ?
Mujhay 'ticket' kidhar se milenge ?
Moojay 'ticket' kiddar say mill-engay ?

How much luggage is allowed ?
Jahāz men kitnā sāman le jā sakte hain ?
Ja-haaz mayn kitnah saamaan lay ja suck-tay highn ?

Can I change my berth ?
Main apnī 'berth' badal saktā hún ?
Maiyn up-nee 'berth' bud-dull suck-tah hoohn ?

When do we arrive ?
Ham kab pahunchenge ?
Hum cub pa-hoohnch-engay ?

112

Put the luggage in my cabin.
Sāmān mere kamray men rakho.
Saamaan may-ray come-ray mayn ruck-oh.

This is the number.
Yah 'number' hai.
.Ya 'number' high.

What are the fares.
Kirāyā kitnā hai.
Kirah-yah kit-nah high.

Do we speak English ?
Ham angrezī bolte hain ?
Hum ung-raziee bowl-tay highn ?

Where is the steward ?
'Steward' kidhar hai ?
'Steward' kiddar high ?

Please prepare my berth.
Merī 'berth' taiyār kījiye.
May-ree 'berth' tie-yaar key-jee-eh.

I feel seasick.
Mujhe chakker ā rahe hain.
Moojay chuck-ker ah rahay highn.

Open the porthole.
Khirkī kholo.
Kir-key kolo.

TRAVEL BY CAR

Car I hire a car here ?
Idhar kirāye par 'car' mil saktí hai ?
Iddar kirah-eh per 'car' mill suck-tea high ?

What does it cost ?
Kirāyā kitnā hai ?
Kirah-yah kit-nah high ?

Is there a petrol station near ?
'Petrol station' nazdík hai ?
'Petrol station' naz-deek high ?

How much per litre ?
'Litre' kā kitnā hai ?
'Litre' kah kit-nah high ?

Give me ten litres.
Mujhe das litre do.
Moojay thus litre doe.

Check the oil.
Tel dekho.
Tail decko.

Fill it up to the level.
Voh púra bharo.
Voh poorah burrow.

Heavy.	Medium	Light
Ghanã.	Madhyam.	Patlã.
Gun-nah.	*Mud-yam.*	*Putt-lah.*

The battery needs charging.
'Battery' ko phir se bharne kí zarúrat hai.
'Battery' ko fear-say burr-nay key zaroo-rut high.

The battery requires water.
'Battery' ko pãní kí zarúrat hai.
'Battery' ko paanee key zaroo-rut high

Put water in the radiator.
'Radiator' men pãní dãlo.
'Radiator' mayn paanee dah-lo.

Service the car.
'Car' sãf karo.
'Car' saaf karo.

Clean the windscreen.
'Car' ke kãch sãf karo.
'Car' kay kaatch saaf karo.

Can we garage the car here ?
Ham 'garage' men 'car' rakh sakte hain ?
Hum 'garage' mayn 'car' ruck suck-tay highn?

Is there a mechanic about ?
Mistrì hai?
Mystery high ?

Look at my brakes.
Brake dekho.
'Brake' decko.

They do not work properly.
Ve ṭhik tarah se nahìn lagte.
Way teak tarah say na-heehn lug-tay.

Give me some air.
Hawa bharo.
Hawāh burxow.

Repair this puncture.
Yah 'puncture' banāo.
Ya 'puncture' bun-aow.

The engine is not running well.
'Engine' ṭhik tarah se nahìn chaltā.
'Engine' teak tarah say na-heehn chall-tah.

It does not pull properly.
Voh ṭhik tarah se nahìn khìnchtā.
Voh teak tarah say na-heehn keench-tah.

It won't go up hills.
Yah pahāriyon par nahín chal sakegā.
Ya pa-ha-ree-ohn per na-heehn chall suck-eh-gah.

Everything is squeaking.

Har ek hissā chín-chín kar rahā hai.

Her-ek hiss-ah cheen-cheen kar ra-hah high.

The doors need oiling.

Darvāzon ko tel chāhiye.

Dervah-zohn ko tail chah-he-eh.

The car has broken down.

'Car' tút gaí hai.

'Car' toot ga-ee high.

Can we get help here?

Idhar kuchh madad mil sakegí ?

Iddar kootch mud-dud mill suck-eh-gee ?

Can we get a tow ?

Hamko rassā mil sakegā ?

Humko russah mill suck-eh-gah ?

Can you lend me a jack ?

'Jack' udhār de sakenge ?

'Jack' ood-daar they suck-engay ?

Can you spare some petrol ?

Āp kuchh 'petrol' de sakenge ?

Aap kootch 'petrol' they suck-engay ?

Go slowly.	**Make haste.**
Dhíre chalo.	Jaldï karo.
Deeray challo.	*Juldy karo.*

Go straight.
   Sídhe chalo.
   See-day challo.

Stop.
   Ruko.
   Rooke.

Turn right.
   Dãyen phiro.
   Dah-ehn fearo.

Turn left.
   Bãen phiro.
   Bah-ehn fearo.

Wait for me here.
   Mere líye idhar ṭhaharo.
   May-ray lee-eh iddar tie-ro.

Wait for me outside.
   Mere liye bãhar ṭhaharo.
   May-ray lee-eh bah-her tie-ro.

Are you free ?
   Ãp ko fursat hai ?
   Aap ko foor-sut high ?

What is the name of this village ?
   Is gãnw kã nãm kyã hai ?
   Iss gaun kah naam kay-aah high?

I wish to leave my car here for tonight.
   Ãj rãt ke liye main apní 'car' idhar chor jãtã
   hún.
   Aaj raat kay lee-eh maiyn up-nee 'car' iddar
   chore ja-tah hoohn.

Is this the way to ...?

....kā rāstā yah hai ?

....kah raas-tah ya high ?

I have lost my way.

Main apnā rāstā kho baithā hún.

Maïyn up-nah raas-tah kho baiyt-ah hoohn.

My car is about 1 km. away.

Merí 'car' lagbhag ek 'kilometre' dúr hai.

May-ree 'car' lug-bug ek 'kilometre' doo-r high.

Please see what is wrong.

Dekhiye to kyā kharābí hai.

Deck-ee-eh toe kay-aah kar-rah-bee high.

Have you spare parts available ?

Ãpke pãs 'car' ke purze mil sakte hain ?

Aap-kay pass 'car' kay poor-zay mill suck-tay highn ?

PARTS OF THE CAR

Lights.

Butti.

But-tea.

Horn.

Bhonpú.

Bom-poo.

Wiper.

Wiper.

Wiper.

Hammer.

Hathaurā.

Ha-tora.

Spot lamp.

Battí.

But-tea.

Spark plug.

Chingārí plug.

Chin-gaaree plug.

ROAD TRAFFIC SIGNS

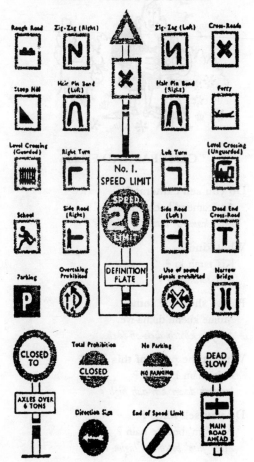

CAMERAS AND FILMS

Do you sell cameras ?
Ãp 'camera' bechte hain ?
Aap 'camera' betch-tay highn ?

What kind ?
Kis tarah ki ?
Kiss tarah key ?

Please show me some.
Mujhe kuchh dikhã-iye.
Moojay kootch dick-ah-ee-eh.

What is the price of this ?
Is kã dãm kyã hai ?
Iss kah daam kay-aah high ?

Do you sell films ?
Ãp 'film' bechte hain ?
Aap 'film' betch-tay highn ?

Movie films too ?
Chala-chitron ke 'film' bhi ?
Challa-chit-rohn kay 'film' bee ?

I want some flash-bulbs.
Mujhe kuchh 'flash-bulb' chāhiye.
Moojay kootch 'flash-bulb' chah-he-eh.

I would like a lightmeter.
Mujhe 'lightmeter' chāhiye.
Moojay 'lightmeter' chah-he-eh.

Can you clean this lens?
Āp yah kāch sāf kar sakenge ?
Aap ya kaatch saaf kar suck-engay ?

Can you repair this shutter?
Yah 'shutter' durust kar sakenge ?
Ya 'shutter' duroost kar suck-engay ?

What is wrong in it ?
Is men kyā kharābī hai ?
Iss mayn kay-aah kar-rah-bee high ?

Would it cost much to repair ?
Durust karne men zyādā paise lagenge kyā?
Duroost kar-nay mayn zey-add-ah pice-ah lug-engay kay-aah ?

Do you develop films ?
Āp 'film' dhote hain ?
Aap 'film ' doe-tay highn ?

How long does it take ?

Is men kitnā wakt lagegã ?

Iss mayn kit-nah wakt lug-eh-gal ?

Can you make enlargements ?

Ãp 'photo' bare kar sakte hain ?

Aap 'photo' bur-ray kar suck-tay highn ?

How much per print ?

'Photo-print' ke kitne paise lete hain?

'Photo-print' kay kit-nay pice-eh lay-tay highn ?

Please finish them quickly.

Ye jaldí banā kar díjiye.

Ye juldy bun-ah kar thee-jee-eh.

These prints are very poor.

Ye 'print' achchhe nahín banãye hain.

Ye 'print' atch-chay na-heehn bun-ah-eh highn.

Have they been over-exposed ?

In par zyãdã roshní dãlí thí ?

In per zey-add-ah rosh-nee dall-ee tea ?

What do you think went wrong ?

Kis bãt men ghalati huí hai ?

Kiss baat mayn gull-tea hoo-ee high ?

What would you suggest ?

Ãp kí salãh kyã hai ?

Aap key salah kay-aah high ?

HUNTING AND SPORTS

India is a paradise for sportsmen. Both small
and big game shooting are among the finest in
the world. Established Shikaris (Hunters), Shops
and Agencies exist in all centres and the tourist
anxious to pursue his favourite sport is well
advised to contact one of these for expert advice.
They will organise a "shoot" for anything from
a tiger to an elephant, sambhar, cheetal, nilgai,
barking deer, sloth bear and wild pig—all come
within their province. They will provide trans-
port, food, beaters, set up camp, skin "the kill"
and arrange for its curing. The technique of shikar
in India can only be acquired by experience and
varies with the terrain and the type of game
sought. It may have to be hunted. It may have
to be stalked. It may require "a drive". It may
require a bait, or it may necessitate long sitting
in a "machan". To do the job properly, one
requires expert advice and it is for this reason
alone that we advise all "would-be killers" to get
in touch with the nearest known and recommended firms specializing in shikar. Any hotel
will point them out. For the fisherman, there is
a wealth of variety. He can fight the mighty
mahseer, or tangle himself with the mighty
goonch which can run up to 300 lbs. He can
float fish for Catla, Rohu, or fly fish for trout.
Fish-filled rivers abound, and local residents are

the best guides to the best spots. Licences are
required for both fishing and shooting, usually
obtained from the local Government authority.
The charges are quite moderate.

CLOTHING

Since most tourists visit India during the winter (cold weather) months November till the end of March, it is advisable to take note of the kind of clothing to bring or buy. Evening and night temperatures drop rapidly, and particularly in Northern India where there is often snow in the Hills. For trips to Northern India therefore, woollen or European clothes are essential, as also wollen underwear. Even in milder regions where hill stations are adjacent, light woollens are advisable. In Maharashtra, the Deccan, and Eastern India, the climate is pleasantly cool and light tropical suiting and cotton or light underwear will suffice.

SPORT : HUNTING AND FISHING

I am a sportsman.
Main khilārī hún.
Maiyn kill-ah-ree hoohn.

I am interested in bird watching.
Main panchhí dekhná chāhtā hún.
Maiyn pun-chee deck-nah chah-ha-tah hoohn.

I want to do some fishing.
Main machhli mārná chāhtā hún.
Maiyn much-lee maar-nah chah-ha-tah hoohn.

I want to shoot small game.
Main chhotā sikhār khelná chāhtā hún.
Maiyn chotah shick-aar kell-nah chah-ha-tah hoohn.

I want to shoot big game.
Main barā shikār khelná chāhtā hún.
Maiyn burrah shick-aar kell-nah chah-ha-tah hoohn.

When does the season open ?
Mausam kab shurú hotā hai ?
Mow-sum cub shooroo hotah high ?

When does the season close ?
Mausam kab khatam hotā hai ?
Mow-sum cub cut-um hotah high ?

Any quail or partridge here ?

Idhar kuchh bater yã títar hain ?

Iddar kootch but-tare ya tea-ter highn ?

Can we shoot green pigeons ?

Ham hare rang ke kabútar mãr sakte hain ?

Hum har-eh rung kay kaboo-ter maar suck-tay highn ?

When can I shoot duck ?

Main battak kab mãr saktã hún ?

Maiyn batack cub maar suck-tah hoohn ?

I would like to bag a jungle cock.

Main janglí murghã pakarnã chãhtã hún.

Maiyn junglee moor-gah pucker-nah chah-ha-tah hoohn.

I suppose we need permits.

Main samajhtã hún ki hamko parwãngí chãhiye.

Maiyn sum-aj-tah hoohn key hum-ko per-waan-gee chah-he-eh.

Where can we get permits ?

Hamko parwãngí kidhar milegí ?

Hum-ko perwaan-gee kiddar mill-eh-gee ?

Do you sell cartridges ?

Tum kãrtús bechte ho ?

Toom car-toos betch-tay ho ?

What is the best time to fish ?

Machhlí mārne kā sab se achchhā wakt
kaunsā hai ?

*Much-lee maar-nay kah sub-say atch-chah wakt
cawn-sah high ?*

I want a light rod.

Mujhe halkí lakrí chāhiye.

Moojay hul-key luck-ree chah-he-eh.

Some fishing line and spoons.

Thorí dor aur chārā.

Tore-ee door owr chah-rah.

What do you recommend ?

Āpkí salāh kyā hai ?

Aap-key salah kay-aah high ?

We shall need beaters.

Hamko dhol bajāne wāle chāhiye.

Humko dole budge-ah-nay wallay chah-he-eh.

We shall require a machan.

Hamko machān chāhiye.

Humko machaan chah-he-eh.

Can you build one for us ?

Tum hamāre liye ek machān banāoge ?

Toom hum-ah-ray lee-eh ek machaan bunaow-gay?

I want to get a tiger.

Main Bāgh kā shikār karnā chāhatā hún.

*Maiyn Baagh kah shick-aar kar-nah chah-ha-ta
·hoohn.*

Give me some cartridges.

Mujhe kuchh kārtús do.

Moojay kootch car-toos doe.

What kind of game is there ?

Udhar kis tarah kā shikār hai ?

Uddar kiss tarah kah shick-aar high ?

There are mosquitoes here.

Idhar machchhar hain.

Iddar much-her highn.

There are many flies here.

Idhar bahut makkhiyān hain.

Iddar ba-hoot muckee-ahn high.

These ants are a nuisance.

Ye chíntiyān āzār haiń.

Ye cheehntee-ahn
ah-zaar highn.

Bring my gun.

Merā bandúk lão.

May-rah bun-dook laow.

Carry my gun.

Merā bandúk le chalo.

May-rah bun-dook lay chailo.

Face the barrel the other way.

Bandúk kí nālí dúsrí taraf karo.

Bun-dook key nah-lee doos-ree ta-ruff karo.

Load my gun.
Bandúk bharo.
Bun-dook burrow.

Do not make any noise.
Shor mat karo.
Shore mut karo.

Is there a beach near here ?
Samundar kā kinārā nazdeek hai ?
Sumoon-der kah kinah-rah naz-deek high ?

Is it safe to swim ?
Idhar tairne men salāmati hai?
Iddar tire-nay mayn salah-matee high ?

Any horse racing going on now ?
Ab ghur-daur chālú hai ?
Ab gore-dowr chah-loo high ?

Whereabout is the race course ?
Ghur-daur kā maidān kidhar hai?
Gore-dowr kah my-dawn kiddar high ?

I would like to play golf.
Main 'golf' khelnā chāhatā hún.
Maiyn 'golf' kell-nah chah-ha-tah hoohn.

Can I get a game of tennis ?
Main 'tennis' khel saktā hún ?
Maiyn 'tennis' kell suck-tah hoohn ?

SPORTS · TERMS

Ammunition.
Bārúd.
Bah-rude.

Bait.
Chārā.
Chah-rah.

Bullet.
Golí.
Goal-ee.

Cartridges.
Kārtús.
Car-toos.

Gun.
Bandúk.
Bun-dook.

Line.
Dor.
Door.

Pistol.
Pistol.
Pistol.

Powder.
Bārúd kā chúrā.
Bah-rude kah choo-rah.

Reel.
Reel.
Reel.

Revolver.
Pistol.
Pistol.

Rifle.
Bandúk.
Bun-dook.

Rod.
Lakrí.
Luck-ree.

Rope.
Rassi.
Russee.

Spoon.
Chārā.
Chah-rah.

ANIMALS

Bat.
Chamgãdar.
Chumgah-der.

Bear.
Ríchh.
Reach.

Bison.
Janglí Bhainsã.
Junglee Baiynsah.

Boar.
Suar.
Sewer.

Buck.
Hiran.
He-run.

Buffalo.
Bhains.
Baiyns.

Bull.
Bail.
Baiyl.

Calf.
Bachhrã.
Batch-rah.

Camel.
Únt.
Oohnt.

Cat.
Billí.
Bill-ee.

Cattle.
Chaupãyã.
Chow-pah-yah.

Cheetah.
Chítã.
Chee-tah.

Cow.
Gãy.
Guy.

Crocodile.
Magar machchh.
Ma-ger-much.

Deer.
Hiran.
He-run.

Dog.
Kuttã.
Cootah.

Donkey.
Gadhã.
Gad-ha.

Elephant.
Hãthí.
Ha-tee.

Fox.
Lomrí.
Lom-ree.

Frog.
Mendak.
Mayn-duck.

Goat.
Bakrí.
Buck-ree.

Hare.
Khargosh.
Kar-gosh.

Hog.
Suar.
Sewer.

Horse.
Ghorã.
Gore-ah.

Lion.
Sher.
Sher.

Mongoose.
Nevalã.
Nay-wallah.

Monkey.
Bandar.
Bun-der.

Mule.
Khachchar.
Kutcher.

Nilgai.
Níl-gãy.
Neel-guy.

Ox.
Bail.
Baiyl.

Panther.
Chítã.
Chee-tah.

Pig.
Suar.
Sewer.

Pony.
Tattú.
Tut-too.

Rabbit.
Khargosh.
Kar-gosh.

Rat.
 Chúhã.
 Choo-ha.

Rhinoceros.
 Gendã.
 Gain-dah.

Scorpion.
 Bichchhú.
 Bitch-choo.

Sheep.
 Bher.
 Bare.

Serpent.
 Sãnp.
 Sahnp.

Snake.
 Sãnp.
 Sahnp.

Squirrel.
 Gilaharí.
 Gilla-heree.

Stag.
 Bãrhã-Singã.
 Bar-ah-sing-ah.

Tiger.
 Chítã.
 Baagh; sher.

Wolf.
 Bheryã.
 Bare-yah.

Moth.
  Patangā.
  Pa-ton-gah.

Sting.
  Dank.
  Dunck.

Silk worm.
  Resham kā kírā.
  Ray-shum kah key-rah.

Wasp.
  Birní.
  Burn-ee.

Spider.
  Makarí.
  Muck-ree.

Worm.
  Kírā.
  Key-rah.

BIRDS, FISH, FOWL GAME

Alligator.
  Magar machchh.
  Ma-ger-much.

Cockatoo.
  Kākātúā.
  Kah-kah-too-ah.

Bird.
  Panchhí.
  Pun-chee.

Crab.
  Kekrā.
  Cake-rah.

Carp.
  Dat̤hi.
  Dar-hee

Crow.
  Kauā.
  Cow-ah.

Chicken.
  Choozā.
  Choose-ah.

Cuckoo.
  Koyal.
  Ko-yal..

Cock
  Murghā.
  Moor-gah.

Dove.
  Kabútar.
  Kaboo-ter.

Duck.
Battak.
Bat-tuck.

Eagle.
Humă.
Hoom-ah.

Eel.
Băm.
Baam.

Fish.
Machhlí.
Much-lee.

Fowl.
Murghă.
Moor-gah.

Goose.
Hans.
Hanse.

Hen.
Murghí.
Moor-gee.

Kite.
Chîl.
Cheel.

Lark.
Chandúl.
Chun-dool.

Lobster.
Jhingă Machhlí.
Jing-ah Muchlee.

Nightingale.
Bulbul.
Buil-buil.

Owl.
Ullú.
Ooloo.

Oyster.
Kastúră.
Kas-toor-ah.

Partridge.
Títar.
Tea-ter.

Parrot.
Totă.
Toe-tah.

Peacock.
Mor.
More.

Pheasant.
Chakor.
Chuck-oar.

Pigeon.
Kabútar.
Kaboo-ter.

Poultry.
 Pāltú murghiyãn.
 Pall-too moor-gee-ahn.

Prawn.
 Jhíngã.
 Jing-ah.

Quail.
 Bater.
 But-tare.

Raven.
 Pahāṛí kauã.
 Pa-ha-ree cow-ah.

Shell-fish.
 Sípdar machlee.
 Sip-dar Much-lee.

Shrimp.
 Jhíngã.
 Jing-ah.

Snipe.
 Chahã.
 Chah-ha.

Sparrow.
 Chiriyã.
 Chiree-ah.

Stork.
 Sãras.
 Sah-russ.

Swallow.
 Abãbíl.
 Abah-beel.

Swan.
 Hans.
 Hanse.

Turkey.
 Filmurgh.
 Fill-moorg.

Vulture.
 Gídh.
 Gidd.

INSECTS

Ants.
Chíntiyãn.
Cheentee-ahn.

Bee.
Madhu-makkhí.
Madoo-muckee.

Beetle.
Gubrílã.
Goo-bree-lah.

Bug.
Khatmal.
Cut-mull.

Butterfly.
Titalí.
Tit-lee.

Caterpillar.
Jhãnjhã.
Jaan-jah.

Centipede.
Kankhajúrã.
Kan-kajoo-rah.

Flea.
Pissú.
Pissoo.

Fly.
Makkhí.
Muckee.

Gnat.
Kutkí.
Koot-key.

Insect.
Kírã.
Key-rah.

Leech.
Jonk.
Johnk.

Lizard.
Chhipkalí.
Chip-kalee.

Locust.
Tíddí.
Tidee.

Louse.
Jún.
Joohn.

Mosquito.
Machchhar.
Much-her.

MAILING AND CORRESPONDENCE

Post and Cable offices are to be found all over India. The villages are served by mobile postal vans, so one can post or receive a letter, send a wire or cable, almost anywhere. When air-mail is used, the sender should, in preference, use only prefranked air-mail paper purchasable at all post offices, or failing that, if the envelope has to be stamped, one should see the stamp defaced in their presence. This is advisable as an extraordinary number of air-mail letters seem never to reach their destination or "go astray en route".

I want to write a letter.

Main chiṭṭhí likhnã chãhatã hún.

Maiyn chit-tea lick-nah chah-ha-tah hoohn.

I want some paper, ink, pen.

Mujhe kuchh kãgaz, syãhí aur kalam chãhiye.

Moojay kootch kah-guz, se-ah-he owr kalam chah-he-eh.

Is there a post box near ?

Dãk kã dabbã nazdík hai ?

Dak kah dub-bah naz-deek high ?

Are there any letters for me ?

Mere liye kuchh chiṭṭhiyãn hain ?

May-ray lee-eh kootch chit-tea-yahn highn ?

Get me some stamps.

Mere liye kuchh 'ticket' le ão.

May-ray lee-eh kootch 'ticket' lay aow.

Where is the post office ?

Dãk-khãnã kidhar hai ?

Dak-kah-nah kiddar high ?

Did you receive my letter ?

Tumko merí chiṭṭhi milí ?

Toomko may-ree chit-tea mill-ee ?

When does the mail leave ?

Dãk kitne baje jãtã hai ?

Dak kit-nay budge-eh jatah high ?

Bring a pen.
  Kalam le āo.
  Kalam lay aow.

What is the date ?
  Kaun-sí tāríkh hai ?
  Cawn-see tah-reek high ?

Seal this letter.
  Yah chiṭṭhí band karo.
  Ya chit-tea bund karo.

I expect some letters.
  Merí kuchh chiṭṭhiyāṅ āne wālí hain.
  May-ree kootch chit-tea-yahn ah-nay wallee highn.

Stick the stamp on.
  'Ticket' lagāo.
  'Ticket' lug-aow.

What is the postage for local letters ?
  Isthāníya chiṭṭhí par kitne 'ticket' lagte hain?
  Iss-taan-ee-ya chit-tea per kit-nay 'ticket' lug-tay highn ?

For abroad ?
  Bāhar ke liye ?
  Bah-her kay lie-eh ?

What is the fee for registration ?
  'Register' karne ke kitne paise hain ?
  'Register' kar-nay kay kit-nay pice-eh highn ?

Is the post office open ?
Dāk-khānā khulā hai ?
Dak-kah-nah kool-ah high ?

When does the mail close ?
Dāk kitne baje band hotā hai ?
Dak kit-nay budge-eh bund hotah high ?

This pen is bad.
Yah kalam kharāb hai.
Ya kalam kar-aab high ?

This paper is poor.
Yah kāgaz sādā hai.
Ya kah-guz sah-dah high.

The gum does not stick.
Gond chipaktā nahín.
Gond chipak-tah na-heehn.

Did you send the letter ?
Tumne chittī bhejí ?
Toom-nay chit-tea bedge-ee ?

Did you stamp it ?
Tumne uspar 'ticket' lagāyā ?
Toom-nay oos-per 'ticket' lugah-yah ?

How long does it take to reach there ?
Udhar pahunchne men kitnā wakt lagtā hai?
Uddar pa-hoohnch-nay mayn kit-nah wakt lug-tah high ?

How many deliveries per day ?
Din men kitní bār dāk miltā hai ?
Din mayn kit-nee bar dak mill-tah high ?

What is the postage for air-mail ?
Hawāī dāk ke liye kitne 'ticket' lagāne parte
hain ?
Ha-wah-ee dak kay lee-eh kit-nay 'ticket' lug-ah-nay per-tay highn ?

How much is ordinary mail ?
Sādhāran dāk ke kitne paise hain ?
Sah-dah-run dak kay kit-nay pice-eh highn ?

How much does an insured letter cost ?
Bímā kí huí chiṭṭhí ke kitne paise hain ?
Bee-mah key hoo-ee chit-tea kay kit-nay pice-eh highn ?

How much is a postcard ?
'Postcard' ke kitne paise hain ?
'Postcard' kay kit-nay pice-eh highn ?

What stamp is needed for a post card ?
'Postcard' per kitne 'ticket' lagte hain ?
'Postcard' per kit-nay 'ticket' lug-tay highn ?

Where is the cable-office ?
Samundarí tār kā daftar kidhar hai ?
Sumoon-deree tar kah daftar kiddar high ?

What is the word rate to London ?
'London' ke liye ek lafz ke kitne paise hain?
'London' kay lee-eh ek luffz kay kit-nay pice-eh highn ?

Here is my message.

Yah mera paighām hai.

Ya may-rah pie-gaam high.

I want to send this parcel.

Main yah 'parcel' bhejnā chāhatā hún.

Maiyn ya 'parcel' bedge-nah chah-ha-tah hoohn.

I want it insured.

Main iskā bímā karānā chāhatā hún.

Maiyn iss-kah bee-mah karah-nah chah-ha-tah hoohn.

Have you a telegram for me ?

Merā tār āyā hai kyā ?

May-rah tar ayah high kay-aah ?

When does it open ?

Voh kitne baje khultā hai ?

Voh kit-nay budge-eh kool-tah high ?

When does it close ?

Voh kitne baje band hotā hai ?

Voh kit-nay budge-eh bund hotah high ?

What is the cost of the bock-post ?

'Book-post' ke liye kitne paise lugte hain ?

'Book-post' kay lee-eh kii-nay pice-eh lug-tay highn?

How much for second class air-mail ?

'Second class' ke hawāī dāk ke kitne paise hain?

'Second-class' kay ha-wah-ee dak kay kit-nay pice-eh highn ?

Can I see the postmaster ?

Main 'postmaster' se mil saktā hún ?

Maiyn 'postmaster' say mill suck-tah hoohn

I want to send a wire.

Main tãr bhejnā chāhatā hún.

Maiyn tar bedge-nah chah-ha-tah hoohn.

Can I phone from here ?

Main idhar se 'phone' kar saktā hún ?

Maiyn iddar say 'phone' kar suck-tah hoohn ?

Where is the box ?

'Telephone' karne ki jagah kidhar hai ?

'Telephone' kay-nay key jug-ah kiddar high ?

What are the fees ?

Kitne paise lagte hain ?

Kit-nay pice-eh lug-tay highn?

Have you a directory ?

Ãp ke pãs 'directory' hai ?

Aap kay pass 'directory' high ?

Can I make a trunk call from here ?

Main idhar se 'trunk call' kar saktā hún.

Maiyn iddar say 'trunk call' kar suck-tah hoohn?

How do I get a connection ?

Mujhe 'connection' kis tarah milegã ?

Moojay 'connection' kiss tarah mill-eh-gah ?

Please deface it.

Is ko radd kíjiye.

Iss-ko rud key-jee-eh.

What does it cost ?
> Is ke kitne paise lugte hain ?
> *Iss kay kit-nay pice-eh lug-tay highn ?*

Here is my identity.
> Yah merí pahachãn hai.
> *Ya may-ree pah-chaan high.*

This is Mr. ....speaking.
> Mr....bol rahe hain.
> *Mr...bowl rahay highn.*

They do not answer.
> Ve jawãb nahín dete.
> *Way jawaab na-heehn they-tay.*

Hold on.
> 'Phone' chãlú rakho.
> *'Phone' chah-loo ruck-oh.*

I shall call back.
> Main phir bulãtã hún.
> *Maiyn fear bull-ah-tah hoohn.*

My number is ...
> Merã 'number' ..hai.
> *May-rah 'number' ...high.*

Will you telephone for me ?
> Ãp mere liye 'telephone' karenge ?
> *Aap may-ray lee-eh 'telephone' kar-engay ?*

I want to make an overseas call.

Main samundar-pār 'phone' karnā chāhatā hūn.

Maiyn sumoon-der-par 'phone' kar-nah chah-ha-tah hoohn.

The line is busy.

'Phone' khālī nahín.

'Phone' call-ee na-heehn.

Will you give him a message ?

Āp usko merā paighām denge ?

Aap oosko may-rah pie-gaam they-engay ?

Ask him to call me.

Us-se kaho ki mujhe bulāe.

Oos-say kaho key moojay bull-ah-eh.

What time will he return ?

Voh kitne baje lautegā ?

Voh kit-nay budge-eh lav-tay-gah ?

How do I dial ?

'Dial' kis tarah phirāún ?

'Dial' kiss tarah fear-ah-oohn ?

I can't get through.

Mujhe nahín ātā.

Moojay na-heehn ah-tah.

Can you connect me with...?

Āp mujhe ....kā 'connection' le denge ?

Aap moojay ...kah 'connection' lay they-engay ?

The telephone is out of order.

'Telephone' <u>kh</u>arāb ho gayā hai.

'Telephone' kar-aab ho gayah high .

May I use your telephone.

Main āp kā 'telephone' kām men lā saktā hún.

Maiyn aap kah 'telephone' kaam mayn lah suck-tah hoohn.

Money order.

Money order,

Money order.

Prepaid.

Pahale diye hue paison wālā.

Pie-lay dee-eh hoo-eh pice-ohn wal-lah.

Special delivery.

Khās pahunch.

Kas pa-hoohnch.

Telegram form.

Tār kā 'form'.

Tar kah 'form'.

How many words ?

Kitne lafz hain ?

Kit-nay luffz highn ?

TERMS

Pen.
Kalam, Pen.
Kalam, pen.

Writing paper.
Likhne kā kāguz.
Lick-nay kah kah-guz.

Envelopes.
Lifāfe.
Lif-ah-fay.

Carbon paper.
Carbon kāgaz.
Carbon kah-guz.

Sealing wax.
Muhar lagāne kí lākh.
Moher lug-ah nay key laak.

Maps.
Nakshe.
Nuck-shay.

String.
Dhāgā.
Dah-gah.

Ink.
Syāhí.
Se-ah-he.

Postcards.
Postcard.
Post card.

Pencil.
Pencil.
Pencil.

Wrapping paper.
Band karne ke liye kāgaz.
Bund kar-nay kay lee-eh kah-guz.

Gum.
Gond.
Gond.

Blotter.
Syāhí-sokh.
Se-ah-he-soak.

Stamps.
Ticket.
Ticket.

Typewriter ribbon.
Typewriter ribbon.
Typewriter ribbon.

TIME AND DAYS OF THE WEEK

What time is it ?
  Kitne baje hain ?
  Kit-nay budge-eh highn ?

Has the clock struck ?
  Ghantā bajā hai kyā ?
  Gun-tah budge-ah high kay-aah.

Set the alarm.
  Ghantī banākar rakho.
  Gun-tea banah kar ruck-oh.

For seven o'clock.
  Sāt baje par.
  Saat budge-eh per.

Wake me early.
  Mujhe sabere jagānā.
  Moojay sub-eh-ray jug-annah.

Look at the time.
  Wakt dekho.
  Wakt decko.

Come tomorrow.
  Kal ānā.
  Kal annah.

Come on Wednesday.
  Budhwār ko ānā.
  Bood-war ko annah.

Come next week.
  Dúsre hafte ānā.
  Doos-ray huff-tay annah.

My watch has stopped.
  Merí gharí ruk gaí hai.
  May-ree gur-ree rook ga-ee high.

My watch is fast.
  Merí gharí āge hai.
  May-ree gur-ree ah-gay high.

The clock has stopped.
  Gharí ruk gaí hai.
  Gur-ree rook ga-ee high.

Is that time correct ?
  Yah wakt thik hai ?
  Ya wakt teak high ?

Am I late ?
  Mujhe der ho gai hai kyā ?
  Moojay they-r ho ga-ee high kay-aah ?

Am I early ?
  Main wakt se pahale āyā hún kyā ?
  Maiyn wakt say pie-lay ayah hoohn kay-ah ?

Is it time to go ?
  Jāne kā wakt huā hai?
  Ja-nay kah wakt hoo-ah high ?

How long will it take ?
  Is men kitnā wakt lagegā ?
  Iss mayn kitnah wakt lug-eh-gah ?

In a short time.
Thore wakt men.
Tore-ay wakt mayn.

In a few days time.
Kuchh dinon ke andar.
Kootch dinohn kay under.

In a week.
Ek hafte men.
Ek huff-tay mayn.

In a month.
Ek mahíne men.
Ek ma-he-nay mayn.

At once.
Ek dam.
Ek dum.

Very Soon.
Bahut jaldí.
Ba-hoot juldy.

Immediately.
Juldí.
Juldy.

Last night.
Kal rät ko.
Kal raat-ko.

Tomorrow afternoon.
Kal dopahar ko.
Kal doe-pahar ko.

Day.
Din.
Din.

Night.
Rät.
Raat.

Morning.
Subah.
Soobah.

Afternoon.
Do-pahar.
Doe-pahar.

Evening.
Shäm.
Shaam.

Midnight.
Ädhí rät.
Ah-dee raat.

Week.
Haftä.
Huff-tah.

Fortnight.
Pakhwärä.
Puck-war-ah.

Month.
Mahínã.
Ma-he-nah.

Year.
Sãl.
Saal.

Today.
Áj.
Aaj.

Tomorrow.
Kal.
Kal.

Hour.
Ghantã.
Gun-tah.

Yesterday.
Kal.
Kal.

Minute.
Minute.
Minute.

Dawn.
Prabhãt.
Pra-baat.

Sun-rise.
Súraj-udaya.
Sooraj-oodayah.

Sun-set.
Súraj-ast.
Sooraj-ast.

Spring.
Bahãr.
Ba-haar.

Summer.
Garmí kã mausam.
Gar-mee kah mow-sum.

Autumn.
Pata-jhar.
Pata-jar.

Winter.
Jãre kã mausam.
Ja-ray kah mow-sum.

Season.
Mausam.
Mow-sum.

Monsoon.
Varshã-kãl.
Vershah-kaal.

It is eight o'clock.
 Āth baje hain.
 Aat budge-eh highn.

Exactly six thirty.
 Púre sãdhe chhe baje.
 Pooray sah-day chay budge-eh.

A quarter past three.
 Savã tín baje.
 Sah-vah teen budge-eh.

Ten minutes till two.
 Do men das 'minute'.
 Doe mayn thus 'minute'.

Five minutes past seven.
 Sãt baj kar panch 'minute.
 Saut budge kar pahnch 'minute'.

Twenty past nine.
 Nau baj kar bís 'minute'.
 Now budge kar beesce 'minute'.

DAYS OF THE WEEK

Monday.
Somwãr.
Soam-war.

Thursday.
Gur-wãr.
Goor-war.

Tuesday.
Maingal-wãr.
Mangal-war.

Friday.
Shukra-wãr.
Shook-ra-war.

Wednesday.
Budh-wãr.
Bood-war.

Saturday.
Shan-wãr.
Shun-war.

Sunday.
Ravi-wãr.
Ravee-war.

MONTHS OF THE YEAR

January.
Pús.
Poos.

July.
Āshārh.
Ah-shahd.

February.
Māgh.
Maag.

August.
Sāwan.
Sah-won.

March.
Phāgun.
Fah-goon.

September.
Bhādon.
Bah-dohn.

April.
Chait.
Chait.

October.
Āshwin.
Aash-win.

May.
Besākh.
Bay-saak.

November.
Kārtik.
Car-tick.

June.
Jeṭh.
Jet.

December.
Agahan.
Agah-hunn.

Note :- The dates of Hindustāní months do not exactly correspond with those of the English months.

THE LAUNDRYMAN

The Indian laundryman (Dhobi - DOE-BEE) is a magician in his own rights. To see him swing your cherished silks and shirts at the riverside where he often does his "washing" is a sight for sore eyes. Beating them monotonously on weatherbeaten rocks is enough to start one's heart palpitating, but lo and behold, instead of beating the garments to shreds, outs they come palpably cleaner, and none the worse (to the eye anyway) for their severe thrashing! This however is a method no longer employed in the bigger and even provincial cities; luckily for the tourist, there and everywhere he will find modern hygienic laundries which can vie with anything abroad and which "do their stuff" to perfection. Quickly and at moderate rates too. However, when one is travelling through the countryside, the "dhobi and washerwoman" can be seen still plying their trade in the old fashioned way - described above.

Have these cleaned and pressed.
Ye dho kar istrí karo.
Ye doe kar isstree karo.

Wash these well.
Ye achchhí tarah dho lo.
Ye atch-chee tarah doe low.

This is not clean.
Yah sǎf nahín nai.
Ya saaf na-heehn high.

Do them again.
Phir se karo.
Fear say karo.

Press these correctly.
Ye thík tarah se istrí karo.
Ye teak tarah say isstree karo.

Where are my socks ?
Mere moze kidhar hain?
May-ray mozay kiddar highn ?

They are still dirty.
Ye abhí tak maile hain
Ye a-bee tuck maiy-lay highn.

Try and get this dirt off.
> Koshish kar yah mail nikāl do.
> *Koshish kar ya maiyl nickaal doe.*

Clean it properly.
> Yah achchhí tarah sāf karo.
> *Ya atch-chee tarah saaf karo.*

The shirt is filthy.
> Kamíz mailí hai.
> *Kameez maiy-lee high.*

Don't use hot water.
> Garam pāní kām men mat lāo.
> *Gar-rum paanee kaam mayn mutt laow.*

The soap is still there.
> Is men abhí sābun hai.
> *Iss mayn a-bee sah-boon high.*

Did you do this ?
> Yah tum ne kiyā ?
> *Ya toom nay key-ah ?*

Rinse them properly.
> Ye achchhí tarah se dho.
> *Ye atch-chee tarah say doe.*

The pocket is torn.
> Jeb phatā huā hai.
> *Jayb fat-ah hoo-ah high.*

Iron them properly.
> Ye achchhí tarah istrí karo.
> *Ye atch-chee tarah isstree karo.*

THE SHOEMAKER

Can you make a pair of shoes for me ?
Tum mere liye júte banā sakte ho ?
Toom may-ray lee-eh jootay bun-nah suck-tay ho?

Like this specimen exactly.
Bilkul isí namúne ke.
Bill-cool issee na-moonay kay.

Can you make a pair of heels ?
Tum eriyăn banā sakte ho ?
Toom ehri-yahn bun-nah suck-tay ho ?

I want new soles for these.
Isko naye tale lagwănā chāhtā hún.
Issko na-yeh talay lug-wah-nah chah-ha-tah hoohn.

Can you have this sewn ?
Yah sí sakte ho ?
Ya see suck-tay ho ?

Have you ready-made shoes ?
Tumhãre pãs taiyãr júte hain ?
Toom-ha-ray pass taiy-aur jootay highn ?

Can I try them on ?
Main pahan dekhún ?
Maiyn pahan deck-hoohn ?

They are much too narrow.
Ye bahut taṇg hain.
Ye ba-hoot tongue highn.

They are far too wide.
Ye bahut bare haiṇ.
Ye ba-hoot burray highn.

The heels are too high.
Erí bahut úṇchí hai.
Ehree ba-hoot oohn-chee high.

Have you got patent leather ?
Tumhãre pãs koí achcbhã chamrã hai ?
Toom-ha-ray pass ko-ee atch-chah chum-rah high?

I want some walking shoes.
Mujhe ghúmne ke wakt kã jutã chãhiye .
Moojay goom-nay kay wakt kah jootah chah-he-eh.

I want some evening shoes.

Mujhe shãm ke liye jútã chãhiye.

Moojay shaam kay lee-eh jootah chah-he-eh.

Can you make golf shoes ?

Tum 'golf' ke júte banã sakte ho ?

Toom 'golf' kay jootay bun-nah sucktay ho ?

I would like them in suede.

Mujhe bakrí ke khãl kã chãhiye.

Moojay buckree key call kah chah-he-eh.

I would prefer sambhar skin.

Mujhe sãmbhar kã chamrã pasand hai.

Moojay sambhar kah chum-rah pasand high.

Can I get crocodile ?

Mujhe magarmachh kã chamrã mil saktã hai ?

Moojay ma-ger-much kah chum-rah mill suck-tah high ?

Will you give me a fit-on first ?

Main pahale pahan kar dek saktã hún ?

Maiyn pie-lay pa-han kar deck suck-tah hoohn ?

When will they be ready ?

Kab taiyãr hogã ?

Cub taiy-aar ho-gah ?

This leather is poor quality.

Yah chamrã sãdã hai.

Ya chumrah sah-dah high.

Let me see better quality.
Koí achchhã chamrã dikhão.
Ko-ee atch-chah chum-rah dick-aow.

Make them just like this.
Bilkul isí tarah banão.
Bill-cool issee tarah bun-naow.

They fit nicely.
Yah bilkul púrã hai.
Ya bill-cool poorah high.

Stretch them just a little.
Yah thorã barã karo.
Ya tore-ah burrah karo.

The stitching is poor.
Silãí achchhí nahíṇ kí hai.
Sillah-ee atch-chee na-heehn key high.

I don't want them like this.
Ye mujhe is tarah nahíṇ chãhiye.
Ye moojay iss tarah na-heehn chah-he-eh.

Show them to me after alteration.
Ṭhík karne ke bãd mujhe dikhão.
Teak kar-nay kay baad moojay dick-aow.

Now they are all right.
Ab yah bilkul ṭhík hai.
Ab ya bill-cool teak high.

THE BARBER

Where is the nearest barber ?
  Idhar sab se nazdík kaun sã hajjãm hai ?
  Iddar subsay nazdeek cawn sah hajjaam high ?

Can you give me a hair cut now ?
  Tum abhí mere bãl banã sakte ho ?
  Toom a-bee may-ray baal banah sucktay ho ?

When can you ?
  Kab banã sakoge ?
  Cub banah suck-oh-gay ?

Do I need an appointment ?
  Wakt mukarrar karne kí zarúrat hai kyã ?
  *Wakt mookar-rer karnay key za-roo-rut high
  kay-aah ?*

Call the barber here.
Hajjām ko idhar bulāo.
Hajjaam ko iddar bull-aow.

Cut my hair please.
Mere bāl banāo.
May-ray baal banaow.

Not too short.
Bahut chhote nahín.
Bahoot chotay na-heehn.

Take off, only a little.
Bahut kam kāṭo.
Ba-hoot come kaato.

Do not touch the top.
Úpar ke bāl mat kāṭo.
Ooper kay baal mutt kaato.

Short at the sides.
Bājú wāle chhoṭe karo.
Baajoo wallay chotay karo.

Not so short in front.
Ãge ki taraf itne chhoṭe mat karo.
Ah-gay key ta-ruff itnay chotay mutt karo.

A little shorter here.
Idhar thore aur chhoṭe karo.
Iddar tore-eh owr chotay karo.

Leave that part alone.
    Sirf voh hissä chhor do.
    Serf voh hissah chore doe.

Trim my beard slightly.
    Merí dãrhi thorì-sì sanwãro.
    May-ree dar-ree tore-ee-see suhnwaaro.

Trim my moustache.
    Merí múchh sanwãro.
    May-ree mootch suhnwaaro.

Do it carefully.
    Khabardãrí se karo.
    Kabardaaree say karo.

Please give me a shave.
    Merí darhí banão.
    May-ree dar-ee banaow.

Shave me clean.
    Ek dam sãf karo.
    Ek dum saaf karo.

Not so close.
    Ultã mat karo—Samãhlo.
    Oolta mutt karo—Sum-ha-lo.

Your razor is blunt.
    Tumhãrã ustarã kund hai.
    Toom-ha-rah oostarah koond high.

It hurts.
Dard hotā hai.
Durd hotah high.

Lather it more.
Zyādā sābun lagāo.
Zey-add-ah sah-boon lugaow.

Sharpen your razor.
Ustarā tez karo.
Oostarah taize karo.

Use clippers.
'Machine' se banāo.
'Machine' say banaow.

Do not use clippers.
'Machine' se mat banāo.
'Machine' say mutt banaow.

I prefer scissors.
Kainchī se banāo.
Kaiyhnchee say banaow.

More off the neck.
Gardan ke bāl aur kāṭo.
Gardan kay baal owr kaato.

Give me a head massage.
Mere sir par mālish karo.
May-ray seer per maalish karo.

Give me a face massage.

Mere múnh par mãlish karo.

May-ray moohn per maalish karo.

I want a shampoo.

Sãbun se mere bãl sãf karo.

Sah-boon say may-ray baal saaf karo.

I do not want a shampoo.

Sãbun se mere bãl sãf mat karo.

Sah-boon say may-ray baal saaf mutt karo.

No hair oil please.

Bãlon men tel mat lagão.

Baal-ohn mayn tail mutt lug-aow.

Part it here.

Idhar mãng nikãlo.

Iddar mahng nicall-oh.

I want my hair washed.

Mere bãl dho dãlo.

May-ray baal doe dall-o.

I want a manicure.

Mujhe hãth aur nãkhúnon ko sajãne wãlã chãhiye.

Moojay haat owr nah-koon-ohn ko sujah-nay walloh chah-he-eh.

Can you give me a tint ?

Tum rang lagã sakte ho ?

Toom rung lugah suck-tay ho ?

The same colour as it is.
　Jaisā yah rang hai, bilkul waisā.
　Jai-sah ya rung high, billcool wai-sah.

What do you suggest ?
　Tumhārī salāh kyā hai ?
　Toom-ha-ree salah kay-aah high ?

A lighter colour.
　Halkā rang.
　Hulkah rung.

A darker colour.
　Gaharā rang.
　Ga-ha-rah rung.

I want a permanent wave.
　Mujhe hameshā ke liye ghunghurāle bāl
　　chāhiye.
　*Moojay hum-eh-shah kay lee-eh goohn-gochn-rah-
　　lay baal chah-he-eh.*

What is the charge ?
　Kitne paise lete ho ?
　Kit-nay pice-eh lay-tay ho ?

Have you any good hair oil ?
　Tumhāre pās koí achchhā bālon kā tel hai ?
　*Toom-ha-ray pass ko-ee atch-chah baal-ohn kah
　　tail high ?*

Can you suggest a new style ?
Tum koí nayã namúnã batã sakte-ho ?
*Toom ko-ee nayah na-moonah batah suck-tay
ho ?*

I would like it bleached.
Is kã rang nikãl ḍalo.
Iss kah rung nicall daal-o.

Do you sell nail varnish ?
Tum 'nail-polish' bechte ho ?
Toom 'nail-polish' baytch-tay ho ?

Do you sell lipsticks ?
Tum 'lipstick' bechte ho ?
Toom 'lipstick' baytch-tay ho ?

THE DOCTOR

I am sick.
Main bímãr hún.
Maiyn bee-maar hoohn.

Call a doctor.
'Doctor' ko bulão.
'Doctor' ko bull-aow.

I have a pain in my stomach.
Mujhe peṭ meṇ dard hai.
Moojay pet mayn durd high.

I have a headache.
Mujhe sir meṇ dard hai.
Moojay seer mayn durd high.

I have fever.
Mujhe bukhãr hai.
Moojay bookaar high.

I have a bad cold.

Mujhe bahut sardí lagí hai.

Moojay ba-hoot sun dee lugee high.

I think I have flu'.

Main samajhtã hún ki mujhe 'flu' hai.

Maiyn sum-aj-tah hoohn key moojay 'flu' high.

I feel giddy.

Mujhe chakkar ã rahe hain.

Moojay chuck-ker ah rahay highn.

I cannot eat.

Main khãnã nahín khã saktã.

Maiyn kah-nah na-heehn kah suck-tah.

I have no appetite.

Mujhe bhúkh nahín lagí.

Moojay book na-heehn lug-tea.

I am constantly vomiting.

Mujhe bahut bãr ulti ãí hai.

Moojay ba-hoot bar ool-tea ah-ee high.

I feel out of sorts.

Mujhe bímãrí-sí mahsús ho rahí hai.

Moojay bee-maaree-see mah-soos ho ra-hee high.

I have a pain here.

Mujhe idhar dard hai.

Moojay iddar durd high.

My legs hurt.

Mujhe tāṅgoṇ men dard hai.

Moojay taang-ohn mayn durd high.

My back hurts.

Mujhe píth men dard hai.

Moojay peet mayn durd high.

My ear aches.

Mujhe kãn men dard hai.

Moojay kaan mayn durd high.

I have constant shivers.

Maiṇ lagãtãr kãmp rahã hún.

Maiyn lug-ah-tar kaamp ra-ha hoohn.

I have pain in the liver.

Mujhe jigar men dard hai.

Moojay jigger mayn durd high.

I have had an accident.

Mere sãth hãdsã húa thã.

May-ray saat haad-sah hoo-ah-tah.

Please examine me.

Merí jãṇch kijiye.

May-ree jahnch key-jee-eh.

Is it broken ?

Yah ṭūṭã huã hai kyã ?

Ya tootah hoo-ah high kay-aah ?

Is it a sprain ?

Moch ã gaí hai kyã ?

Motch ah ga-ee high kay-aah ?

I have a constant itch.

Mujhe lagātār khujlī ho rahī hai.

Moojay lug-ah-tar koojlee ho ra-hee high.

I find difficulty in breathing.

Mujhe sāns lene men taklīf hotī hai.

Moojay sahns laynay mayn tuck-leaf ho-tee high.

Must I go to hospital ?

Mujhe aspatāl men jānā chāhiye kyā ?

Moojay us-pataal mayn ja-nah chah-he-eh kay-aah?

Can't you look after me ?

Āp merā ilāj nahīn kar sakte ?

Aap may-rah ill-laaj na-heehn kar sucktay ?

Please send me some medicine.

Kuchchh dawā bhejiye.

Kootch dawah bedge-ee-eh.

How long will it take ?

Is men kitnā wakt lagegā ?

Iss mayn kitnah wakt lug-eh-gah ?

Shall I be all right ?

Kya main thīk ho jāūngā ?

Kay-aah maiyn teak ho ja-oongah ?

How often should I take this ?

Yah kitnī bār lenī chāhiye ?

Ya kitnee bar laynee chah-he-eh ?

How much shall I take ?
   Mujhe kitní lení chãhiye ?
   Moojay kitnee laynee cha^h-he-eh ?

I feel nauseated.
   Ultí kã wichãr ho rahã hai.
   Ool-tea kah witchaar ho ra-ha high.

Everything looks dim.
   Har chíz dhúndhulí dikhãi detí hai.
   Her cheese doohndlee dick-ah-ee they-tea high.

I need some aspirin.
   Mujhe kuchchh 'Aspirin' chãhiye.
   Moojay kootch 'Aspirin' chah-he-eh.

I need quinine.
   Mujhe 'Quinine' chãhiye.
   Moojay 'Quinine' chah-he-eh.

I must buy iodine.
   Mujhe 'Iodine' lenã chãhiye.
   Moojay 'Iodine' lay-nah chah-he-eh.

I have a high temperature.
   Mujhe bahut zor kã bukhãr hai.
   Moojay ba-hoot zore kah bookaar high.

Low in the mornings.
   Subah ko kam hotã hai.
   Soobah ko come hotah high.

High at night time.

Rãt ko zyãdã hotã hai.

Raat ko zey-add-ah hotah high.

Must I stay in bed ?

Mujhe bistar men rahnã chãhiye kyã ?

Moojay bister mayn ra-ha-na chah-he-eh kay-aah?

Can't I get up occasionally ?

Kyã, kabhí kabhí mujhe uṭhnã na chãhiye?

Kay-aah, kabee kabee moojay ootnah na chah-he-eh ?

Can you fill this prescription ?

Yah nuskhã likh denge ?

Ya nooss-kah lick they-engay ?

Can you give me something to rub in ?

Ãp kuchchh lagãne ke liye denge ?

Aap kootch lug-ah-nay kay lee-eh they-engay ?

Give me something for insect-bites.

Kíron ke kãṭne par lagãne ke liye kuchchh
dawã díjiye.

*Key-rohn kay kaat-nay per lug-ah-nay kay lee-eh
kootch dawah thee-jee-eh.*

MEDICAL TERMS

Accident.
Hãdsã.
Haad-sah.

Allergy.
Allergy.
Allergy.

Appetite.
Bhúkh.
Book.

Bandage.
Pattí.
Putt-tea.

Blister.
Phapholã.
Fafo-lah.

Blood.
Khún.
Koon.

Boil.
Phorã.
Forah.

Breath.
Dam; Sãns.
Dam; Sahns.

Chill.
  Sardí.
  Sur-dee

Cholera.
  Haizã.
  High-zah.

Cold.
  Zukãm; Sardí.
  Zoo-calm; sur-dee.

Colic.
  Pet kã dard.
  Pet kah durd.

Constipation.
  Kabz.
  Kabz.

Corn.
  Ghatthã.
  Gattah.

Cough.
  Khãnsí.
  Kahnsee.

Cramp.
  Maror.
  Muroar.

Diarrhoea.
  Dast.
  Dust.

Diet.
  Khurãk.
  Kooraack.

Digestion.
  Hãzmã.
  Haaz-mah.

Disease.
  Bímãrí.
  Bee-ma-ree.

Drugs.
  Dawã.
  Dawah.

Dysentery.
  Pechish.
  Pay-chish.

Ear-ache.
  Kãn kã dard.
  Kaan kah durd.

Emetic.
  Julãb.
  Joolaab.

Epilepsy.
  Mirgí.
  Mirgee.

Exhaustion.
  Thakãwat.
  Tuckah-wat.

Fainting.
  Behoshí.
  Bay-ho-she.

Fatigue.
  Thakãwat.
  Tuck.ah-wat.

Fever.
  Bukhãr.
  Bookaar.

Gout.
  Gathiyã.
  Gutt-tee-yah.

Gravel.
  Pathrí.
  Putter-ee.

Headache.
  Sir dard.
  Seer-durd.

Hoarseness.
  Ãwãz kã bhãrípan.
  Ah-waaz kah bah-ree-pun.

Indigestion.
  Badhazmí.
  Bud-hazmee.

Infection.
  Phahalne wãlí bímãrí.
  Fa-hal-nay wallee bee-maaree.

Itch.
  Khujlí.
  Koojlee.

Jaundice.
  Píliyã.
  Peelee-ah.

Leprosy.
  Korh.
  Core.

Liver.
  Jigar.
  Jigger.

Measles.
  Mãtã.
  Ma-tah.

Medicine.
  Dawã.
  Dawah.

Nausea.
  Mitlí.
  Mit-lee.

Ointment.
Marham.
Mur-hum.

Pain.
Dard.
Durd.

Paralysis.
Lakwā.
Luck-wah.

Perspiration.
Pasínā.
Pus-seenah.

Piles.
Bawāsír.
Bawah-seer.

Pimples.
Phunsí.
Foon-see.

Plague.
Wabā.
Wabah.

Poison.
Zahar.
Za-her.

Poultice.
Lep.
Lay-p.

Purgative.
Julāb.
joolaab.

Remedy.
Ilāj.
Ill-laaj.

Ringworm.
Dād.
Daad.

Small-pox.
Barí mātā.
Burry ma-tah.

Swelling.
Sújan.
Soojun.

X-ray.
X-ray.
X-ray.

Wound.
Zakhm.
Zakm.

THE DENTIST

Where can I find a good dentist ?

Koí achchhā dãnton kā 'doctor' kidhar
milega ?

*Ko-ee atch-chah dahnt-ohn kah 'doctor' kiddar
mill-eh-gah ?*

Is he fully qualified ?

Voh achchhā jãnkăr hai ?

Voh atch-chah jaan-car high ?

Abroad or locally ?

Bãhar se síkh kar ãyã hai yã idhar se ?

Bah-her say seek kar ayah high ya iddar say ?

This tooth hurts.

Is dant men dard hai.

Iss dahnt mayn durd high.

My gum gives me pain here.

Idhar masúron men dard hai.

Iddar musoorohn mayn durd hai.

The filling has fallen out.

Ãp ne jo bharã thã voh nikal gayã hai.

Aap nay jo burrah tah voh nickal gayah high.

Can you fill it now ?

Yah ab bharoge ?

Ya ab burro-gay ?

I have a swelling here.

Mujhe idhar súyan hai.

Moojay iddar soojan high.

Must you take it out ?

Kyã yah nikãlnã hí hogã ?

Kay-aah ya nickaalnah he hogah ?

Give me a pain killer.

Mujhe dard mitãne wãlí dawã do.

Moojay durd mitah-nay wallee dawah doe.

Can you do it now ?

Kyã abhí kar sakenge ?

Kay-aah abee kar suck-engay ?

Clean my teeth, please.

Mere dant sãf kíjiye.

May-ray dahnt saaf key-jee-eh.

183

It hurts continuously.

Is men lagãtãr dard hotã hai.

Iss mayn lugah-taar durd hotah high.

Give me some tooth-drops please.

Dant men dãlne kí kuchh dawã díjiye.

Dahnt mayn dall-nay key kootch dawah dee-jee-eh.

And some cotton-wool.

Aur thorí kapãs.

Owr tore-ee kapass.

I have an abscess.

Mujhe pípdãr phorã hai.

Moojay peep-daar forah high.

I have broken my denture.

Mere naklí dãnt tút gaye hain.

May-ray nucklee dahnt toot ga-eh highn.

Can you repair it ?

Ãp ye banã sakenge ?

Aap ye banah suck-engay ?

Give me an anaesthetic.

Mujhe chamrí ko behosh karne walí dawã
    díjiye.

*Moojay chum-ree ko bay-hosh kar-nay wallee
    dawah thee-jee-eh.*

This molar hurts me.

Is dãrh men dard hai.

Iss daarh mayn durd high.

My gums bleed frequently.
Masúron se kaí bãr khún nikaltã hai.
Musoorohn say ka-ee bar koon nickal-tah high.

BANKING AND COMMERCIAL TERMS

BANKING

All the major foreign banks have their own branch offices or correspondents throughout India. In some places, the systems are a bit out-of-date and cashing a cheque can be a tedious experience. In all these matters, one should always remember that in journeying throughout the whole of this vast continent, one can only "hasten slowly".

MONEY, CURRENCY

Every person arriving in India MUST furnish a Currency Declaration if he has any currency with him. This will enable him to take out, without difficulty, any that he is left with at the time of his departure. No person is permitted to bring into India more than Rs.75 in Indian currency, but he may bring in an unlimited amount of foreign currency which he must, however, declare at the time of his entry. Travellers cheques need not be declared.

Although India follows the decimal system of coinage, the older and better known "anna" is still quoted. The Rupee is divided into 100 paise (formerly 16 annas). But the present as well as the former subdivisions are quoted below:

Rupee	Paise	Annas
1.00	100	16
0.50	50	8
0.25	25	4

An approximate idea of the equivalent value of the Rupee in British, Swiss, French, Russian and American currencies is as follows :

Rupee	Pound	Swiss Franc	French Franc	Russian Rouble	Dollar
100	7.10.6	91/40	102.5	18.9	21/15
1	1/6	92cts.	1.02F.S	18 Rs.	21 cts.

Where is the nearest bank ?

Idhar nazdík kaun-sã 'bank' hai ?

Iddar naz-deek cawn-sah 'bank' high ?

I have a bank draft.

Mere pãs 'draft' hai.

May-ray pass 'draft' high.

I have this cheque.
Mere pãs yah 'cheque' hai.
May-ray pass ya 'cheque' high.

I have a letter of credit.
Mere pãs hundí hai.
May-ray pass hoondee high.

Do you take dollars ?
Ãp 'dollar' lete hain kyã ?
Aap 'dollar' laytay highn kay-aah ?

What is the rate of exchange ?
Paisã badalne kã bhãv kyã hai ?
Pice-ah bud-dull-nay kah baav kay-aah high ?

I have travellers cheques with me.
Mere pas sailãniyon ke 'cheque' hain.
May-ray paas sailannee-ohn kay 'cheque' highn.

Will you cash this please ?
Ap yah tor denge ? (or) - Ãp iske paise denge ?
Aap ya tore they-engay ? (or) - Aap isskay pice-eh they-engay ?

(Please) give me rupees in exchange.
Mujhe badle men rupae dijiye.
Moojay budlay mayn roopee-eh thee-jee-eh.

Please give me large notes.
Mujhe bare 'note' díjiye.
Moojay burray 'note' thee-jee-eh.

Please give me small notes.
Mujhe chhoṭe 'note' díjiye.
Moojay chotay 'note' thee-jee-eh.

Some small change (please).
Thorí rezgí díjiye.
Torz-ee rezy-gee thee-jee-eh.

COMMERCIAL TERMS

Account.
Hisáb-kitáb.
Hisaab-kitaab.

Advance.
Peshgí.
Paysh-gee.

Agreement.
Ikrár.
Ick-raar.

Amount.
Paisá.
Pice-ah.

Auction.
Nílám.
Nee-laam.

Balance.
Báki.
Bah-key.

Banker.
Sarráf.
Ser-raaf.

Bargain.
Mol-tol; Saudá.
Mole-tole; Sowdah.

Bill.
Hundí.
Hoondee.

Bond.
Dastáwez.
Dustah-ways.

To borrow.
Karz lenã.
Kurz lay-nah.

Broker.
Dallãl.
Dull-all.

Brokerage
Dallãlí.
Dull-all-lee.

Bullion.
Sone yã chãndí kí
ínt.
*Sonay ya chahndee key
eehnt.*

Business.
Vyãpãr.
Vee-ah-par.

Buyer.
Kharídãr.
Karee-daar.

Capital.
Púnjí.
Poohnjee.

Cargo.
Bojh.
Bodg.

Cashier.
Khazãnchí.
Kazaan-chee.

Cash.
Nakd.
Nakad.

Change.
Rezgí.
Rays-gee.

Cheque.
Hundí.
Hoondee.

Commerce.
Vyãpãr.
Vee-ah-par.

Commission.
Dallãlí.
Dull-all-lee.

Condition.
Shart.
Shirt.

Consign.
Hawãle karnã.
Ha-wah-lay kar-nah.

Contract.
Ṭhekã.
Take-ah.

Cotton.
  Kapãs.
  Kapass.

Credit
  Sãkh; udhãr.
  Saak; ood-aar.

Creditor.
  Lendãr.
  Lane-dar.

Crop.
  Fasl.
  Fussal.

Currency.
  Sikkã; 'note'
  Sickah; 'note'.

Current.
  Chãlú.
  Chah-loo.

Customer.
  Kharídãr.
  Karee-daar.

Customs.
  Mahsúl.
  Ma-ha-sool.

Debt.
  Karz.
  Karz.

Debtor.
  Karzdãr.
  Karz-daar.

Dealings.
  Len-den.
  Lane-den.

Demand.
  Mãng.
  Maang.

Department.
  Vibhãg.
  Vibaag.

Deposit.
  Amãnat.
  Amah-nut.

Discount.
  Katautí.
  Cutow-tea.

Dividend.
  Munãfã.
  Moonah-fah.

Draft.
Hundí.
Hoondee.

Duty.
Mahsúl.
Ma-ha-socl.

Expenses.
Kharch.
Kartch.

Export.
Rawãngí.
Ra-wahn-gee.

Factory.
Kãr khãnã.
Car-kah-nah.

Firm.
'Firm' ;
kothí.
'Firm'; kotea.

Freight.
Kirãyã.
Kirah-yah.

Gain.
Munãfa.
Moonah-fah.

Goods.
Sãmãn.
Saamaan.

Import.
Ãyãt.
Ah-yaat.

Insurance.
Bímã.
Bee-mah.

Interest.
Súd.
Sood.

Lease.
Pattã.
Putt-tah.

Letter of Credit.
Hundi.
Hoondee.

Letter of exchange.
Muddat kí hundí.
Moodut key hoondee.

Loan.
Karz.
Karz.

Loss.
Nuksãn.
Nook-saan.

Marks.
  Nishãn.
  Nishaan.

Merchant.
  Saudagar.
  Sow-dah-ger.

Mortgage.
  Girwí.
  Gir-wee.

Office.
  Daftar.
  Daftar.

Partner.
  Hissedãr.
  Hisseh-daar.

Partnership.
  Hissedãrí.
  Hisseh-dah-ree.

Profit.
  Nafã.
  Nuffah.

Property.
  Milkiyat.
  Milkee-at.

Purchase.
  Kharídãrí.
  Karee-dah-ree.

Ra e.
  Bhãw.
  Baau.

Receipt.
  Rasíd.
  Ruseed.

Retail.
  Phutkar-bikrí.
  Footkar-bickree.

Sample.
  Namúnã.
  Na-moon-ah.

Shop.
  Dúkãn.
  Dookaan.

Sign.
  Sahí.
  Sa-hee.

Signature.
  Sahí.
  Sa-hee.

Stamp-paper.
  Stãmp kã kãghaz.
  Stamp kah kah-gaz.

Trade.
  Vyãpãr.
  Vee-ah-par.

Warehouse.
Kothí.
Kotea.

Wholesale.
Thok.
Toak.

Weight.
Wazan.
Wazan.

PLACES AND OBJECTS YOU MAY WISH TO SEE IN TOWN AND COUNTRY

Aboriginals.
Ãdivãsí.
Ah-dee-va-see.

Building.
Imãrat.
Imah-rut.

Bank.
Bank.
Bank.

Canal.
Nahar.
Na-her.

Battlefield.
Jaŋg kã maidãn.
Jung kah maiy-dawn.

Capital.
Rãjdhãní.
Raaj-dah-nee.

Bridge.
Pul.
Pool.

Caravan.
Kãflã.
Calf-lah.

Cave.
Gufā.
Goofah.

Cemetery.
Makbarā.
Muck-burrah.

Church.
Girjā ghar, 'Church'.
Girjaw-gar, 'Church'.

Citadel.
Kilā.
Kill-ah.

City.
Shahar.
Shah-her.

Coal mine.
Koyale kí khān.
Ko-eh-lay key kaan.

College.
College,
Mahāvidyālaya.
College,
Ma-ha-videe-ah-lah.

Court.
Kachahrí.
Kutch-cherry.

Γ ocks.
Bandargāh.
Bunder-gaah.

Γome.
Makbarā.
Muck-burrah.

Factory.
Kārkhānā.
Car-kah-nah.

Falls.
Jharnā.
Jer-nah.

Farm.
Khet.
Kate.

Fort.
Kilā.
Kill-ah.

Forest.
Jangal.
Jungle.

Fountain.
Chashmā.
Chash-mah.

Garden.
Bagíchā.
Bug-ee-chah.

Gate.
Darwāzā.
Der-wah-zah.

Goldfields.
Sone kí khānen.
Sonay key kaan-ehn.

Government house.
Rājbhavan.
Raaj-bawan.

Grave.
Kabar.
Kaber.

Guest house.
Mehmān khānā.
Mayh-maan-kah-nah.

Harbour.
Bandargāh.
Bunder-gah.

Hill.
Pahārí.
Pa-ha-ree.

Hotel.
Hotel.
Hotel.

Hospital.
Aspatāl.
Uspataal.

House.
Ghar.
Gar.

Hut.
Jhonprí.
Jowhnpree.

Lake.
Tālāb.
Talaab.

Lane.
Galí.
Gullee.

Law court.
Kachahrí.
Kutch-cherry.

Library.
Kutub-khānā.
Kootoob-kah-nah.

Light house.
Roshan-minār.
Roshun-minaar.

Machan.
Machān.
Mah-chaan.

Market.
Bāzār.
Bazaar.

Mint.
Ţaksāl.
Tuck-scal.

Mine.
Khān.
Kaan.

Monument.
Yādgār.
Yaadgaar.

Mosque.
Masjid.
Musjid.

Museum.
Ajāyab ghar.
A-jaw-yub-gar.

Orchard.
Bāgh.
Baug.

Painting.
Chitra, Taswír.
Chitra, Tasweer.

Palace.
Mahal.
Mahal.

Palanquin.
Pālkí.
Paal-key.

Pier.
Khambhā.
Come-bah.

Pillar.
Khambhā.
Come-bah.

Police station.
Thānā.
Thah-nah.

Post office.
Ḍāk khānā.
Dak-kah-nah.

Prison.
Jel khānā.
Jail-kah-nah.

Quarry.
Patthar kí khān.
Putter key kaan.

Ravine.
Ghātí.
Gaatee.

Reservoir.
Tālāb, Hauz.
Talaab, Howz.

Resthouse.
Ārām-ghar.
Ah-raam-gar.

River.
  Nadí.
  Nadee.

Ruins.
  Khandahar.
  Kand-her.

School.
  Vidyālaya; Madarsā.
  *Videe-ah-lah; Mother-
    sah.*

Sculpture.
  Múrtí kalā.
  Moortee kalah.

Shops.
  Dúkānen.
  Dookaanehn.

Springs.
  Jharnā.
  Jer-nah.

Square.
  Chauk.
  Chowk.

Statue.
  Putlā.
  Poot-lah.

Steamer.
  Āgbút.
  Aag-boot.

Steeple.
  Mínār.
  Meenaar.

Street.
  Galí.
  Gullee.

Tank.
  Tālāb.
  Talaab.

Temple.
  Mandir,
  Mundeer.

Theatre.
  Nātak ghar.
  Nah-tuck gar.

Throne.
  Takht.
  Tukt.

Tomb.
  Makbarā.
  Muck-burrah.

Tower.
  Ghantā ghar.
  Guntah-gar.

Town.
  Shahar.
  Shah-her.

Treasury.
Khazānā.
Kazah-nah.

University.
Vidyā-píth.
Videe-ah-peet.

Tribes.
Kaumen.
Quo-mayn.

Village.
Gānw.
Gawhn.

Well.
Kuāṇ.
Koo-ahn.

MINERALS, METALS AND PRECIOUS STONES

Alum.
Phitkari.
Fit-karee.

Amber.
Ambar.
Amber.

Brass.
Pital.
Peatal.

Bronze.
Kānsā.
Kansaw.

Cement.
Cement.
Cement.

Charcoal.
Koyalā.
Ko-eh-lah.

Chalk.
Chāk.
Chalk.

Clay.
Mitti
Mit-tea.

Coal.
Koyalā.
Ko-eh-lah.

Copper.
Tāmbā.
Taam-bah.

Coral.
Mungā.
Moon-gah.

Crystal.
Billaur.
Bill-owr.

Diamond
Hirā.
Heerah.

Emerald.
Pannā
Pun-nah.

Glass.
Shishā, kāch.
Sheshah, Kaatch.

Gem.
Jawāhar.
Jawah-her.

Gold.
Sonã.
Sonah.

Gravel.
Ret, kankar.
Rate, kan-ker.

Iron.
Lohã.
Low-ha.

Lead.
Sísã.
See-saw.

Lime.
Chúnã.
Choonah.

Lapis Lazuli.
Nílam Lãjaward.
Neelum Laajwerd.

Marble.
Sangmarmar.
Sungmurmur.

Manganese.
Manganese.
Manganese.

Mercury.
Pãrã.
Par-ah.

Metal.
Dhãtú.
Dah-too.

Mica.
Abrak.
Ab-ruck.

Mortar.
Gãrã, gach.
Gah-rah, gatch.

Opal.
Dúdhiyã patthar.
Doodee ah putter.

Pearl.
Motí.
Motea.

Precious stone.
Ratna.
Ra-ton.

Ruby.
Lãl, yãkút.
Laal, yah-koot.

Sapphire.
Nílam.
Neelum

Silver.
Chãndí.
Chahn-dee.

Steel.	**Sulphur.**
Faulād.	Gandhak.
Fow-laad.	*Gun-duck.*
Stone.	**Tin.**
Patthar.	Kalaí, Tín.
Putter.	*Kala-ee, Teen.*

Iron ore.
Kacchā lohā.
Kutchah low-ha.

ARTICLES IN COMMON DAILY USE

Ashtray.
Rākh dăn.
Raak-daan.

Bandage.
Patti.
Putt-tee.

Basket.
Tokrí.
Tokree.

Bedding.
Bistar.
Bister.

Beer mug.
Beer mug.
Beer mug.

Bottle opener.
Botal kholne kā ozăr.
Bottle kolany kah o-zaar.

Box.
Petí.
Pay-tea.

Bracelet.
Bazu-band.
Bah-zoo-bund.

Bulb.
Bulb.
Bulb.

China.
Chíní ke bartan.
Cheenee kay burr-ton.

Clock.
Gharí.
Gurree.

Cloth.
Kaprā.
Cup-rah.

Compact.
Singar kí petí.
Singaar key pay-tea.

Comb.
Kanghā.
Kangah.

Cork.
Dăt.
Daat.

Cork screw.
Dăt kholne kā ozăr.
Daat kolnay kah o-zaar.

Cufflinks.
Cufflinks.
Cufflinks.

Cushion.
Gaddí.
Gaddee.

Deodorant.
Badbú mitănewălí
chíz.
*Budboo mitah-nay
wallee cheese.*

Doll.
Guriyă.
Goo-ree-ah.

Earrings.
Kăn ke zevár.
Kaan kay zaywer.

Embroidery.
Zar-dozí.
Zar-dozee.

Face powder.
Face powder.
Face powder.

Flash light.
Flash light.
Flash light.

Flit.
Flit.
Flit.

Hair brush.
Bălon kă 'brush'
Baal-ohn kah 'brush'

Hair pins.
Balon ke kănte.
Baal-ohn kay kahntay.

Hand bag.
Chhoṭí bag.
Chotea bag.

Hot-water-bottle.
Garam pắní kí botal.
*Gar-rum paanee key
bottle.*

Hydrogen peroxide.
Hydrogen peroxide.
Hydrogen peroxide.

Ice.
Barf.
Ba-ruff.

Ice bag.
Barf kí thailí.
Ba-ruff key thaiy-lee.

Insect cream.
　Insect cream.
　Insect cream.

Insect Repellant.
　Kirã mãrne wãlí
　　dawã.
　Key-rah maar-nay
　　wallee dawah.

Iodine.
　Iodine.
　Iodine.

Iron.
　Istrí.
　Iss-tree.

Jewellery.
　Zewar.
　Zay-wer.

Lace.
　Patti.
　Putt-tee.

Laxative.
　Julãb.
　Joolaab.

Leather.
　Chamre kí patti.
　Chum-ray key
　　putt-tee.

Linen.
　Kaprã.
　Cup-rah.

Lint.
　Patti.
　Putt-tee.

Lipstick.
　Lipstick; surkhí.
　Lip stick; Soor-key.

Mirror.
　Ãinã.
　Ah-ee-nah.

Mosquito net.
　Machchhardãní.
　Mucher-dah-nee.

Mouth wash.
　Munh sãf karne kí
　　dawã.
　Moohn saaf kar-nay
　　key dawah.

Nailfile.
　Nãkhún banãne ki
　　retí.
　Nah-koon bananay key
　　raytea.

Necklace.
　Hãr.
　Haar.

Needle.
Suí.
Soo-ee.

Notebook.
Notebook.
Notebook.

Ointment.
Marham.
Mur-hum.

Penknife.
Chhoṭā chākú.
Chotah chah-koo.

Perfume.
Itra; khushbú.
Attar; kooshboo.

Safety pin.
Safety pin.
Safety pin.

Pin.
Pin.
Pin.

Print.
Chhāp.
Chaap.

Radio.
Radio.
Radio.

Razor.
Ustarā.
Oos-tarah.

Razor blades.
Dārhí banāne ke
'blade'.
*Dar-ree bananay kay
'blade'.*

Record.
Record.
Record.

Ring.
Angúthí.
Ungoo-tea.

Rubber.
Rubber.
Rubber.

Rug.
Kambal.
Come-bal.

Sedative.
Dard mitāne wālí
dawā.
*Durd mitah-nay
wallee dawah.*

Scissors.
Kainchí.
Kaiyhnchee.

Screws.
Pech.
Petch.

Shampoo.
Bāl dhone kí dawā.
Baal doe-nay key dawah.

Silk.
Resham.
Ray-shum.

Silverware.
Chāndí ke bartan.
Chahn-dee kay burrton.

Smelling salts.
Smelling salts.
Smelling salts.

Souvenirs.
Yādgār.
Yaad-gaar.

Stones.
Kímtí patthar.
Key-mat-ee putter.

Sun-cream.
Dhúp kí cream.
Doop key cream.

Sun-glasses.
Dhúp kā chashmā.
Doop kah chash-mah

Table-cloth.
Mez-posh.
Maize-poash.

Thermometer.
Thermometer.
Thermometer.

Thimble.
Angushtar.
Ungoosh-ter.

Thread.
Dhāgā.
Dah-gah.

Tooth brush.
Tooth brush.
Tooth brush.

Tooth paste.
Tooth paste.
Tooth paste.

Toys.
Khilaune.
Kill-own-nay.

Trunks.
Petiyān.
Pay-tea-ahn.

Umbrella.
Chhátá.
Chaatah.

Wood.
Lakrí.
Luck-ree.

Vase.
Phúldán.
Fool-daan.

Wood carving.
Káth Nakkáshí.
Kaat Nuck-kah-she.

Wire.
Tár.
Tar.

Wool.
Ún.
Oon.

THE HINDUSTANI LANGUAGE

The contents of the Phrase Book are printed in the colloquial form of the Hindustani language, the language of the masses in India, as spoken and understood almost in every part of the country. Due to the British influence in India, Indian languages are greatly influenced by the English language. You will thus find various English words used in colloquial forms of many Indian languages. Hindustani is not an exception to this fact. The Hindustani translations given in this book do not aim at giving the corresponding Hindustani word for each and every English word. Such English words which are current in colloquial Hindustani and are spoken and understood even by those who do not know the English language, are incorporated in the Hindustani translation without any hesitation. No purpose would be served by giving such Hindustani words in translation which are coined by scholars, and which when spoken by the tourist would not be understood by the people of this country.

The following grammatical facts will help the reader to know some of the peculiarities of Hindustani:

1. Nouns:- There are two genders in Hindustani - masculine and feminine. There is no neuter gender. Thus all nouns show any of these two genders. All inanimate objects are either masculine or feminine in Hindustani grammar.

Hindustani nouns show two numbers - singular and plural. The plural number is generally shown by adding different suffixes.

2. Pronouns:- Hindustani pronouns do not show gender distinction except in the possessive case. Possessive pronouns show the gender distinction according to the gender of the noun with which they are related, e.g:

Merā Betā	"My son"
Merí Betí	"My daughter"

Most of the Hindustani pronouns distinguish singular and plural.

3. Adjectives:- Hindustani adjectives ending in-ā, undergo change according to the nouns with which they are related. Other adjectives generally remain unchanged, e.g:

Achchhā larkā	"Good boy"
Achchhí larkí	"Good girl"
But, Sundar larkā	"Handsome boy"
Sundar larkí	"Beautiful girl"

4. Verbs:- Hindustani verbs are different from English verbs in this respect that they show masculine or feminine gender.

Larkă jãegă   "A boy will go"
Larki jãegí   "A girl will go"

The rules underneath are applicable to all Hindustani verbs.

The infinitives of verbs in Hindustani end in Nā such as "to go"… "jãnã"; "to come"…"ãnã".

Drop "nã" and add "o" and you get the Imperative, such as "go" …"jão" ; "come"…"ão".

Similarly drop "nã" and add "tã" and you get the present participle such as "going"… "jãtã"; "coming"… "ãtã".

Finally when you drop "na" and add "ã" you get the past tense or past participle such as "gone"… "gaya"; "came"… "ãyã".

FUTURE TENSE
Singular

He will speak.
Voh bolegā.
Voh bowl-eh-gah.

He will come.
Voh āegā.
Voh ah-eh-gah.

He will go.
Voh jāegā.
Voh ja-eh-gah.

He will bring.
Voh lāegā.
Voh lah-eh-gah.

Plural

They will speak.
Ve bolenge.
Way bowl-engay.

They will come.
Ve āenge.
Way ah-engay.

They will go.
Ve jāenge.
Way ja-engay.

They will bring.
Ve lāenge.
Way lah-engay.

5. Prepositions :- Hindustani prepositions, in fact, should be called postpositions. In English the preposition occurs before the word with which it is related. But in Hindustani, it occurs after the word:

Hāth *men*   "*In* hand"

6. Adverbs, Conjunctions and Interjections:- Most of the Hindustani adverbs do not undergo any change. Hindustani conjunctions and

interjections, as in the English language, always
remain unchanged.

7. Sentences:- The usual pattern of the Simple
sentence in Hindustani is as follows:-

SUBJECT - OBJECT - VERB
(A boy eats a mango).

Larkā	ām	khātā hai.
Larkah	*aam*	*kahtah high.*

| A boy | mango | eats |

CARDINAL NUMBERS

One	Eleven	Thirty
Ek	Gyārah	Tís
Ek	*Gay-arah*	*Teese*
Two	Twelve	Forty
Do	Bārah	Chālís
Doe	*Bah-rah*	*Chah-leese*
Three	Thirteen	Fifty
Tín	Terah	Pachās
Teen	*Tay-rah*	*Patch-aas*
Four	Fourteen	Sixty
Chār	Chaudah	Sāth
Char	*Chow-dah*	*Saath*
Five	Fifteen	Seventy
Pānch	Pandrah	Sattar
Pahnch	*Pand-rah*	*Sat-ter*
Six	Sixteen	Eighty
Chhe	Solah	Assí
Chay	*Sole-ah*	*As-see*
Seven	Seventeen	Ninety
Sāt	Satrah	Nabbe
Saat	*Sat-rah*	*Nab-bay*
Eight	Eighteen	Hundred
Āṭh	Aṭṭhārah	Sau
Aat	*At-taarah*	*Sow*
Nine	Nineteen	Thousand
Nau	Unís	Hazār
Now	*Oon-eece*	*Haz-aar*
Ten	Twenty	(100,000)
Das	Bís	Lākh
Thus	*Beesce*	*Laak*

Examples of other cardinal numerals :-

Twenty-five
 Pachchis
 Patch-chees

Forty-five
 Paintālís
 Pentah-leese

Thirty-one
 Ikatís
 Ika-teese

Eighty-four
 Chaurāsí
 Chow-rah-see

ORDINAL NUMBERS

First
 Pahala
 Pie-lah

Sixth
 Chathã
 Cha-tah

Second
 Dúsrã
 Doos-rah

Seventh
 Sātvãn
 Saat-vahn

Third
 Tísrã
 Teese-rah

Eighth
 Āthvãn
 Aat-vahn

Fourth
 Chautha
 Chow-tah

Ninth
 Nauvãn
 Now-vahn

Fifth
 Pãnchvãn
 Pahnch-vahn

Tenth
 Dasvãn
 Thus-vahn

The Ordinals after the fourth are formed by adding '-vahn' to the cardinals, with the exception of Sixth.

FRACTIONAL NUMBERS

A Quarter (¼)
  Pãv
  Paav

Half (½)
  Ãdhã
  Ah-dah

Three quarters (¾)
  Paunã
  Pown-nah

One and three quarters (1¾)
  Paune do
  Pown-nay-doe

One and a quarter (1¼)
  Savã
  Sah-vah

Two and a quarter (2¼)
  Savã do
  Sah-vah-doe

One and a half (1½)
  Dedh
  Dead

Two and a half (2½)
  Adhãí
  Ad-hai

Three and a half (3½)
  Sãdhe tín
  Saad-hay teen

(Pown-nay), (Sah-vah) and (Saad-hay) are similarly added to other numbers.

USEFUL VERBS

To abuse
Gālí denā
Gaalee theynah

To accept
Kabúl kernā
Kabool kar-nah

To answer
Javāb denā
Ja-vaab theynah

To arrive
Pahunchnā
Pa-hoohnch-nah

To ask
Púchhnā
Pooch-nah

To bathe
Guhsal karnā
Goose-al kar-nah

To become
Honā
Honah

To beat
Māmā
Maar-nah

To begin
Shurú karnā
Shocroc kar-nah

To believe
Mānnā
Maan-nah

To break
Tornā
Tore-nah

To bring
Lānā
Lah-nah

To buy
Kharídnā
Kareed-nah

To carry
Le jānā
Lay ja-nah

To change
Badalnā
Bud-dull-nah

To choose
Pasand karnā
Pasand kar-nah

To clean
Sāf karnā
Saaf kar-nah

To clothe
Kapre pahannā
Cup-ray pa-han-nah

To come
Ānā
Annah

To conceal
Chhipānā
Chip-ah-nah

To cook
Pakānā
Puckah-nah

To cry
Ronā
Ronah

To cut
Kātnā
Kaat-nah

To dance
Nachnā
Naatch-nah

To decline
Inkār karnā
In-kaar kar-nah

To die
Mar jānā
Mer ja-nah

To dig
Khodnā
Kod-nah

To dine
Khānā khānā
Kah-nah kah-nah

To do
Karnā
Kar-nah

To doubt
Shak karnā
Shak kar-nah

To drink
Pínā
Pee-nah

To drive
Hānknā
Hahnk-nah

To eat
Hānknā
Hahnk-nah

To eat
Khānā
Kah-nah

To enjoy
Khushí manānā
Kooshee manah-nah

To explain
Samjhānā
Sum-ja-nah

To except
Umed rakhna
Oomaid rak-nah

To fall
Gir jānā
Gir ja-nah

To fear
Darnā
Dar-nah

To feed
Khilānā
Kill-ah-nah

To fight
Larnā
Lar-nah

To finish
Púrā karnā
Poorah kar-nah

To follow
Píchhe jānā
Peech-chay ja-nah

To forget
Bhúl jānā
Bool ja-nah

To forgive
Māf karnā
Maaf kar-nah

To gain
Hāsil karnā
Haasil kar-nah

To get up
Uthnā
Oot-nah

To give
Denā
Theynah

To go
Jānā
Ja-nah

To go in
Andar jānā
Under ja-nah

To go up
Upar jānā
Ooper ja-nah

To go out
Bāhār jānā
Bah-her ja-nah

To go back
Vāpas jānā
Wah-pus ja-nah

To go away
Chale jānā
Challay ja-nah

To hear
Sunnā
Soon-nah

To hide
Chhipānā
Chip-ah-nah

To hire
Kirāye par lenā
Kirah-eh per laynah

To hold
Pakamā
Pucker-nah

To hope
Umed karnā
Oomaid kar-nah

To inform
Khabar denā
Kabar theynah

To invite
Bulānā
Bull-ah-nah

To jump
Kudnā
Kood-nah

To keep
Rakhnā
Rak-nah

To know
Jānnā
Jaan-nah

To laugh
Hansnā
Hans-nah

To learn
Sīkhnā
Seek-nah

To light
Silgānā
Silgah-nah

To like
Pasand karnā
Pasand kar-nah

To live
Rahnā
Ra-ha-nah

To lose
Khonā
Konah

To make
Banānā
Banana

To marry
Shādí karnā
Shaadee kar-nah

To meet
Milnā
Mill-nah

To mix
Milānā
Mill-ah-nah

To mount
Charhnā
Char-nah

To move
Hilnā
Hill-nah

To obey
Hukum mānnā
Hookum maan-nah

To open
Kholnā
Kol-nah

To play
Khelnā
Kell-nah

To please
Khush karnā
Koosh kar-nah

To prepare
Taiyār karnā
Tie-yaar kar-nah

To prevent
Roknā
Roknah

To print
Chhāpnā
Chaap-nah

To punish
Sazā denā
Sazah theynah

To put
Rakhnā
Rak-nah

To quarrel
Lamā
Lar-nah

To read
Parhnā
Purr-nah

To remember
Yād karnā
Yaad kar-nah

To repair
Marammat karnā
Maram-mat kar-nah

To rest
Ārām karnā
Ah-raam kar-nah

To return
Phirānā
Fear-ah-nah

To rise
Uthnā
Oot-nah

To run
Daurnā
Dour-nah

To run away
Bhāg jānā
Baag ja-nah

To say
Kahanā
Ka-ha-nah

To search
Dhūndhnā
Doohnd-nch

To see
Dekhnā
Deck-nah

To sell
Bechnā
Betch-nah

To send
Bhejnā
Bedge-nah

To serve
Naukri karna
Nowkree kar-nah

To sew
Sinā
Seenah

To show
Dikhānā
Dick-ah-nah

To shut
Band karnā
Bund kar-nah

To sing
Gānā
Gah-nah

To sit
Baiṭhnā
Bait-nah

To sleep
Sonā
Sonah

To smell Súnghnā *Soong-nah*	**To take** Lenā *Lay-nah*
To smoke Tambākú pína *Tambaakoo peenah*	**To teach** Sikhānā *Sick-ah-nah*
To speak Bolnā *Bowl-nah*	**To tear** Phārnā *Far-nah*
To spend Kharch karnā *Karch kar-nah*	**To think** Sochnā *Sotch-nah*
To spit Thúknā *Thook-nah*	**To throw** Phenknā *Fenk-nah*
To stand Kharā rahanā *Karah ra-ha-nah*	**To tie** Bāndhnā *Baand-nah*
To steal Churānā *Choor-ah-nah*	**To travel** Safar karnā *Suffer kar-nah*
To strike Mārnā *Maar-nah*	**To try** Koshish karnā *Koshish kar-nah*
To swim Tire nāh *Tire-nah*	**To turn** Phirānā *Fear-ah-nah*

To understand
Samajhnā
Sum-aj-nah

To wake
Jagānā
Jagah-nah

To wait
Thaharnā
Tie-her-nah

To want
Chāhnā
Chah-ha-nah

To wash
Dhonā
Doe-nah

To walk
Chalnā
Chal-nah

To wear
Pahannā
Pa-han-nah

To weigh
Tolnā
Tole-nah

To work
Kām karnā
Kaam kar-nah

To worship
Pujā karnā
Poojah kar-nah

To write
Likhnā
Lick-nah

ADJECTIVES FOR DAILY USE

Active
Chālāk
Chah-laak

Angry
Gusse
Gus-say

Any
Koí
Ko-ee

All
Sab
Sub

Another
Dúsrā
Doos-rah

Bad
Kharāb
Kar-aab

Beautiful
Sundar
Soon-der

Better
Behtar
Bai-ter

Bitter
Kadvā
Karvah

Blind
Andha
Un-dah

Brave
Bahādur
Bah-hah-dur

Broad
Chaurā
Chow-rah

Both
Donon
Doe-nohn

Careful
Khabardār
Kabar-daar

Cheap
Sastā
Sas-tah

Clean
Sāf
Saaf

Clever
Hoshyār
Hosh-yaar

Cold
Thandā
Ton-dah

Common
Ãm
Aam

Cruel
Berahm
Bay-ra-hum

Deaf
Baharā
Bai-rah

Dear (costly)
Mahangā
Ma-hengah

Difficult
Mushkil
Moosh-kill

Dirty
Maila
My-lah

Dishonest
Be-ímān
Bay-eemaan

Dry
Súkhā
Sook-hah

Dusty
Mailā
My-lah

Early
Jaldí
Juldy

Easy
Ãsãn
Ah-saan

Empty
Khālí
Kah-lee

Equal
Barābar
Ba-rah-ber

Every one
Har koi
Her ko-ee

Every
Har
Her

False
Jhúthā
Jute-hah

Famous
  Mashahúr
  Masha-hoor

Fat
  Mota
  Moat-ah

Few
  Thorã
  Tore-ah

Fine
  Umdã
  Oom-dah

First
  Pahalã
  Pie-lah

Fit
  Lãiq
  Lah-ick

Foolish
  Bevakúf
  Bay-va-koof

Free
  Ãzãd
  Ah-zaad

Fresh
  Tãzã
  Taazah

Gay
  Khush
  Koosh

Gentle
  Sharíf
  Sha-reef

Glad
  Khush
  Koosh

Good
  Achchhã
  Atch-chah

Great
  Barã
  Burrah

Happy
  Khush
  Koosh

Hard
  Sakht
  Sakt

Hasty
  Utãvalã
  Ootah-valah

Healthy
  Tandurust
  Tand-roost

Heavy
Bhārī
Bah-ree

High
Únchā
Oontchah

Honest
Ímāndār
Eemaan-daar

Hot
Garam
Gar-rum

Hungry
Bhúkhā
Book-hah

Ill
Bímār
Bee-maar

Important
Zarúrī
Zarooree

Innocent
Be-gunāh
Bay-goonah

Just
Insāf-pasand
Insaaf-pasand

Lame
Langrā
Lung-rah

Last
Ākhirīn
Aak-reen

Large
Barā
Burrah

Late
Der-se
Dare-say

Lazy
Sust
Soost

Lean
Patlā
Putt-lah

Light
Halkā
Hal-kah

Like this
Aisā
Ai-sah

Like that
Vaisā
Vai-sah

Like which
Jaisā
Jai-sah

Like what
Kaisā
Kai-sah

Long
Lambā
Lumbah

Loose
Dhilā
Deelah

Lucky
Khush-nasíb
Koosh-naseeb

Mad
Dívānā
Dee-wannah

Much
Bahut
Ba-hoot

Naked
Nangā
Nun-gah

Narrow
Tang
Tongue

Necessary
Zarúrí
Zarooree

New
Nayā
Na-yah

Old
Purānā
Poorah-nah

Open
Khulā
Kool-lah

Poor
Gharíb
Gareeb

Present
Hāzir
Ha-zir

Private
Khāngí
Kaan-gee

Proud
Maghrúr
Mag-roor

Pure
Sāf
Saaf

Quiet	**Sharp**
Chup	Tez
Choop	*Taize*
Raw	**Short**
Kachchã	Chhotã
Kutch-chah	*Chhtah*
Ready	**Slow**
Taiyãr	Ãhistã
Tie-yaar	*Ah-hiss-tah*
Rich	**Small**
Daulat-mand	Chhotã
Dowlat-mand	*Chotah*
Right	**Soft**
Durust	Narm
Duroost	*Nar-rum*
Ripe	**Some**
Pakkã	Kuchh
Pukkah	*Kootch*
Round	**Some other**
Gol	Dúsrã koí
Goal	*Doos-rah ko-ee*
Sad	**Sorry**
Udãs	Dilgír
Oo-daas	*Dil-geer*
Separate	**Sour**
Judã	Khattã
Judah	*Kat-tah*

Straight	**This**
Sídhã	Yah
Seed-hah	*Ya*
Strong	**This much**
Maz-bút	Itnã
Maz-boot	*It-nah*
Sweet	**Tight**
Míthã	Tang
Meetah	*Tongue*
Tall	**Tired**
Lambã	Thakã huã
Lumbah	*Thakah hoo-ah*
That	**True**
Voh	Sachchã
Voh	*Such-chah*
Their	**Ugly**
Unkã	Bad-súrat
Oon-kah	*Bud-soorat*
Thick	**Unfit**
Moṭã	Nã-lãik
Moat-ah	*Nah-lah-ick*
Thin	**Useful**
Patlã	Kãm-kã
Putt-lah	*Kaam-kah*
Thirsty	**Useless**
Pyãsã	Nikammã
Pea-ah-sah	*Nick-come-ah*

Warm	**Wrong**
Garm	Ghalat
Gar-rum	*Gull-at*
Weak	**Whatever**
Kamzor	Jo kuchh
Come-zore	*Jo kootch*
Wet	**Whoever**
Gîlā	Jo koí
Geelah	*Jo ko-ee*
Whole	**Young**
Púrā	Javān
Poorah	*Ja-vaam*
Wild	**Your**
Janglí	Tumhārā
Jung-lee	*Toom-ha-rah*
Wise	
Sayānā	
Say-ah-nah	

IMPORTANT ADVERBS, CONJUNCTIONS AND PREPOSITIONS

(Those which appear in the Basic Vocabulary have been omitted from this section.)

After	Always
Bād	Hameshā
Baad	*Hum-eh-sha*

Again	And
Phir	Aur
Fear	*Our*

Against	At first
Khilāf	Pahale
Kilaaf	*Pie-lay*

Almost	At last
Lag-bhag	Ākhir
Lug-bug	*Aakir*

Alone	Because
Akelā	Kyún-ki
Akay-lah	*Queon-key*

Also	Before
Bhí	Āge
Bee	*Ah-gay*

Although	Behind
Agar-che	Píchhe
Agerch	*Pea-chey*

Below	**From**
Níche	Se
Neechay	*Say*
Between	**How many ?**
Bích men	Kitne ?
Beech mayn	*Kit-nay ?*
But	**If**
Lekin	Agar
Lay-kin	*Agar*
Certainly	**Immediately**
Zarúr	Fauran
Zaroor	*Fow-run*
Enough	**In**
Bas	Men
Bus	*Mayn*
Except	**Instead**
Sivã	Ke badle
Sivah	*Kay budlay*
Far	**Less**
Dúr	Kam
Doo-r	*Come*
For	**More**
Ke vaste	Zyãdã
Kay vaastey	*Zey-add-ah*
Formerly	**Near**
Pahale	Nazdík
Pie-lay	*Naz-deek*

Never
Kabhí nahín
Kabee na-heehn

Seldom
Kabhí kabhí
Kabee kabee

Not at all
Kabhí nahín
Kabee na-heehn

Some times
Kabhí kabhí
Kabee kabee

Now
Ab
Ab

Suddenly
Achănak
Achah-nak

No where
Kahín nahín
Kaheehn na-heehn

Then
Tab
Tub

Of
Kã (m); kí (f)
Kah; key

There
Udhar
Uddar

On
Par
Per

Therefore
Isí liye
Iss-see lee-eh

Only
Sirf
Sirf

Thus
Aisã
Ai-sah

Or
Yã
Yah

To
Ko
Ko

Perhaps
Shãyɘd
Shah-yad

Together
Sãth
Saath

Towards
Taraf
Ta-ruff

Under
Níche
Neechay

Undoubtedly
Be-shak
Bay-shak

Until
Jab tak
Jab tuck

Upon
Par
Per

Very
Bahut
Ba-hoot

When ?
Jab ?
Jub ?

Where ?
Jahān ?
Ja-hahn ?

Why ?
Kyún ?
Queon ?

With
Ke sāth
Kay saath

Without
Sivā
Sivah

Yes
Hān
Hahn